WHILE BRITAIN SLEPT

WHILE BRITAIN SLEPT

The Selling Of The Common Market

by

DOUGLAS EVANS

LONDON
VICTOR GOLLANCZ LTD
1975

ISBN 0 575 02018 0

MADE AND PRINTED IN GREAT BRITAIN BY
THE GARDEN CITY PRESS LIMITED
LETCHWORTH, HERTFORDSHIRE
SG6 1JS

*Dedicated to my father,
George Morton Evans,
with great affection and respect*

ACKNOWLEDGMENTS

A book of this kind is inevitably the unconscious outgrowth of my experience, observations and convictions of several years, but especially of the last five when I have been writing about the EEC and its external consequences. During this time I have been influenced by many people, some of them intimately involved in the running of the Community, others profoundly affected by it.

To each of these people I acknowledge their often unconscious help in the formation of my ideas and attitudes on the subject of this book. I would like in addition to acknowledge the assistance given me by several people in particular in the compilation of this account. They include, on the Conservative Party, the Rt. Hon. the Earl of Avon, Edward Holloway, and the Rt. Hon. J. Enoch Powell; on the Labour Party, the Rt. Hon. Tony Benn, William Pickles and the Rt. Hon. Lord Wigg; on the Civil Service, Lord Armstrong and Lord Greenhill.

On a very practical level I wish to acknowledge the help and encouragement I have received from my agent, Andrew Best of Curtis Brown; also the entire staff of Victor Gollancz for having pushed my book through with such rapidity in collaboration with The Garden City Press but especially to my editor John Richard Pearce (who also husbanded my two previous symposia, *Destiny or Delusion* and *Britain in the EEC*), and latterly Liz Calder. Finally, I wish to thank Viviane Asher who belongs to that very select band of people who are able to read my handwriting, and who typed the greater part of the manuscript.

While much of this book has been gleaned from direct sources who wish to remain anonymous and almost all the official documents and minutes pertaining to the period will not be available for some years, it would be ungracious if I did not give some prominence to the debt I owe to the most substantive work on the subject I chose to write about, Dr Uwe Kitzinger's *Diplomacy and Persuasion*. While I began this book some time before Dr Kitzinger's book was published it was inevitable that we should record many of the same events though with, in general, markedly different conclusions. It is a tribute to Dr Kitzinger's fairness that despite his active commitment to British entry he has not suppressed evidence that reflects awkwardly on some of the aspects of the campaign to bring about entry.

In his own words, Dr Kitzinger has provided "a quarry and a tool for research" which anyone writing upon the subject in the future cannot ignore.

CONTENTS

Great Britain has lost an empire and has not yet found a role.
Dean Acheson (1962)

Men ought not to suffer from disenchantment: they ought to know that ideals in politics are never realized.
William Ewart Gladstone (1891)

PREFACE

AFTER A DECADE of setting her face towards entry Britain finds herself a full member of the European Economic Community and beginning to face the implications in every area of her national life. It is arguable that not since the decade 1680 to 1690, when the Glorious Revolution was enacted, has Britain undergone such a radical shift in political, constitutional and commercial power. Though there may be arguments about the precise nature of national sovereignty at a given moment, there can be little argument that entry greatly reinforced and accelerated the transfer of power from parliamentary to non-parliamentary institutions. Whether these national and supra-national bureaucracies are situated in London or Brussels, whether they are government ministries, multinational companies, transnational trade unions, or even cabinets or councils of ministers, they are in practical terms either wholly or partially unaccountable to parliamentary control. For notwithstanding the gradual diminution of parliamentary authority in the post-war period the sovereignty of Parliament had, up to the moment of British entry, at least remained constitutionally, if not actually, intact and therefore presumably capable of resuscitation.

The remarkable fact is that this radical realignment of power and accountability took place without Common Market entry ever being treated as a clear-cut election issue. Rather than submitting individual policies for approval, historically British governments have usually sought general mandates. They have nevertheless usually indicated where they stood on major national issues. In the case of the Common Market neither of the two major political parties observed this practice in any of the three General Elections of 1964, 1966 or 1970; on the contrary they made sure that the Common Market was a non-issue at each of these elections, even though first the Labour Government in 1967 and then the Conservative Government in 1970 were to make entry a central objective of their respective administrations. In the case of the Conservatives it was to become the overriding objective. The deliberate exclusion of any form of popular involvement in the decision-making about British entry has been as striking in its way as the American people's exclusion from the decision-making process over Vietnam. It is the assumption that foreign policy is somehow beyond the concern and comprehension of the British people that this book sets out to challenge.

There are inevitably some basic questions that need answering. Were Britain's democratic institutions by-passed completely, were they subverted, or did they merely operate according to customary processes which are less democratic than we fondly imagine? Clearly, with an issue of such magnitude there have been pressure groups at work both in Britain and abroad and a great deal of money, imagination and effort has been expended. The question is, which are the main pressure groups and how precisely have they operated? One of the assumptions that has been made in this book is that Britain being a traditional country with venerable democratic institutions, each with an equally venerable mythology with which to gild themselves, the most influential pressure groups have by and large tended to operate discreetly within the traditional institutions. The body of the book is in fact an attempt to describe how those institutions worked over the course of the 1960s and 1970s in relation to a particular major issue, namely whether Britain should or should not join the Common Market.

I

THE CONSERVATIVE PARTY

BEFORE EXAMINING THE behaviour of the Conservative
Party towards the EEC since it came into being in 1958, it is
necessary to relate the history of the party's relations with
Western Europe in the immediate postwar period and especially
the role that its leaders played in the process of European
recovery and integration. To understand that the Conservative
leaders wished to encourage European unity without themselves
feeling the necessity to commit Britain other than in a supporting
role is something quite fundamental to any true appreciation of
the British role in the first postwar decade. The most apt summary of the British position at this time was expressed by Lord
Avon in his memoirs, *Full Circle* (Cassell; p. 29): "We continu-
ously encouraged close co-operation and unity between the
continental powers but we did so from the reserve position that
we would not accept a sovereign European authority... Others
found this outlook patronizing and irritating... [but] we have
a different and distinct outlook.... It is because as a people we
like to proceed by trial and error. We prefer to see how a principle works in practice before we enshrine it, if we ever do so."

Just as twenty years later Kennedy was more universally
admired abroad than he was by his own people, at least in his
lifetime, so Churchill stood as a heroic champion of individual
and national liberty in the eyes of most postwar West Europeans,
regarded as of even greater stature on the Continent than he
was at home. With characteristic eloquence Churchill gave a
famous speech at Zurich in September 1946 in which he spoke
of the goal of "a kind of United States of Europe", a view which
he reinforced in another celebrated oration at the Hague Congress of May 1948. Continental "Europeans" clutched at his
statements—here was someone who could act as a standard
bearer for their cause. In fact, while he proclaimed the need for
European unity and Britain's willingness to promote that aim,
he always ruled out Britain's integration into a European union,
as his Zurich speech made plain when he bracketed Britain and

the Commonwealth, along with the United States and, he hoped, the Soviet Union, as "friends and sponsors of the new Europe". Nevertheless the Conservatives, largely because they were in opposition and could afford to adopt the task of putting forward general aspirations rather than blueprints that they had no power to introduce, gradually built up a reputation among many Continental "Europeans" that they were more committed to concrete European involvements than the Labour Government. This was not too difficult during the period that Ernest Bevin was at the Foreign Office as he consistently pursued a policy of Britain first.

It was in the spring of 1950 that the French Foreign Minister, Robert Schuman, took the first significant step forward in the process of Franco-German postwar collaboration and West European integration when he proposed that the pooling of Franco-German coal and steel production should be placed under a common "higher authority" which would be open to other countries in Europe. As he then expressed it, "this was to be the first step in the federation of Europe". Britain was invited to join the negotiations but predictably refused. It was not only the supporters of Ernest Bevin who had fears about British participation in the Schuman Plan. As Harold Macmillan, a long-time "European" who had helped to establish the Council of Europe and was ultimately to lend his support to the Schuman Plan, said at the time : "One thing is certain, and we may as well face it. Our people will not hand over to any supranational authority the right to close down our pits or our steelworks." It was the difference in attitude between nations that had been conquered and ravaged and those that had not, between those peoples who had a folk memory of three Franco-Germanic wars on their territory and those who could look back over a thousand years of independent existence. The European Coal and Steel Community Treaty was signed by the Six in April 1951 and came into operation in July 1952. Parallel to the ECSC was an attempt to create a European Defence Community.

The background to the EDC was fairly clear cut. In 1950 the NATO powers could only muster fourteen divisions on the Continent to match the 175 Soviet divisions. When the Korean War broke out in July the situation had become so serious that by September, at a meeting of the North Atlantic Council in New York, the United States, in the person of Secretary of State Dean Acheson, called for German rearmament and threatened to withdraw from Europe if this was not accomplished. At the same time there were deep fears of a revival of German militarism, most of all by the French who demanded cast-iron safeguards. In response to these two conflicting requirements the Pleven Plan was presented to the French National Assembly on 25 October 1950 and was accepted. Basically it involved three new elements: first the creation of a European army comprised of national units integrated at the smallest unit possible; second, a European Defence Minister responsible to a European Assembly and a European Defence Council of Ministers; and thirdly a single European Defence Budget. As always in Western Europe's long history of internal conflict it was only when the external threat was most imminent that such far-reaching schemes for European integration were mooted by political leaders. The whole concept of a supranational body with very considerable powers leading to a permanent federal set of institutions was quite foreign to British aspirations as Ernest Bevin put it to the House of Commons on 29 November. He added: "Europe is not enough; it is not big enough, it is not strong enough, and it is not able to stand by itself. It is this great conception of an Atlantic Community that we want to build up." His attitudes were widely supported on the Conservative benches. However, plans for a direct German contribution to NATO were to fail. And when Herbert Morrison succeeded Bevin on the latter's death the EDC was seen as the only means of achieving German rearmament. Then in September Morrison, Secretary of State Acheson and the French Foreign Minister, Schuman, issued a joint declaration of support for the EDC. There was nonetheless a notable absence of any promise of direct British participation. There was in fact an acceptance by all three signatories that Britain, while lending her certain support to the French, would make no direct contribution to the European Army.

All of these elements were to be retained and carried over by the Conservatives when they returned to power at the end of October 1951. This was made quite explicit by the new Foreign Secretary, Anthony Eden, in his speech to the House of Commons of 19 November:

"His Majesty's Government promise their whole-hearted support to the development of this European community [i.e. the Schuman Plan and the EDC] within a constantly growing Atlantic community.

"In this connection there is no doubt that the declaration of the three Foreign Ministers at Washington on September 14th marked a considerable step forward. We endorse that declaration."

From this background it may be fairly gleaned that the views of the Tory leadership were not at this point that much different from their Labour predecessors in office. It is true that Winston Churchill had suggested at Strasbourg in August 1950 "that we should make a gesture of practical guidance by declaring ourselves in favour of the immediate creation of a European army under a unified command and in which we shall bear a worthy and honourable part". But this was in advance of the announcement of the Pleven Plan with its quite unacceptable federal proposals. Lord Normanbrook, Secretary to the Cabinet, confirms that Churchill "was particularly distressed by the plans for a European Army; an integrated organization of the kind then envisaged would not, in his view, provide an effective fighting force".[1]

If Churchill always rejected the EDC along the lines envisaged by the French in favour of an Atlanticist defence force, then Eden certainly did so too. Thus in his speech to the House of Commons of 29 November he said :

"It may well be that the Atlantic grouping will be the one in which our forces will mainly lie. It does not exclude some contribution perhaps to the European Army, if my conception of it is the right one. . . ." Like Churchill, Eden seems to have supported the EDC not because he especially valued its general design but because it seemed one of the few means available, apparently acceptable in principle to both the Germans and the French. It is also clear that he always doubted whether it would succeed and feared the results of its proving a failure. The Churchill-Eden position on the EDC, that of support from the outside, seems to have accurately reflected the majority of opinion not only within the Conservative Party but also in the Commons and among the electorate at this time. It was also shared by the Supreme Commander of NATO in Europe, General Eisenhower, who told Eden on 22 November that "Britain should help from without rather than participate from within".[2]

In a personal minute to the Prime Minister, Eden wrote on 1 December that the British Government should support the

---

[1] Ed. Sir John Wheeler-Bennett, *In Action This Day*, p. 41.
[2] Lord Avon, *Full Circle*, Cassell, p. 33.

Pleven Plan but not become members, adding significantly: "This is what the Americans are doing, and it is the course Eisenhower wants us to take." Moreover, if the Pleven Plan collapses we should "try to work out a more modest scheme with our allies . . . without an elaborate political superstructure". Any aim to modify the Pleven Plan will need to be timed carefully as "we shall be told we have killed it". The above summary of an Eden memo is of considerable significance as indicating the feeling of the Conservative Government for the next three years. As we shall see, it was only when the Plan had failed, thrown out by the French National Assembly, that Eden initiated an alternative scheme. On 11 May 1953 Churchill expressed the Conservative Government's attitude towards the EDC and the evolving European integration movement quite precisely:

"We are not members of the European Defence Community, nor do we intend to be merged in a Federal European system. We find we have a special relation to both. This can be expressed by prepositions, by the preposition 'with' but not 'of'—we are with them but not of them. We have our own Commonwealth and Empire . . ."

Meanwhile, back on 1 February 1952, Eden put action to support his words of "the closest possible association" by informing M Schuman of a speech he was about to make to the House of Commons. It contained a general proposal that Britain should establish the closest political and military links with the EDC. It included further proposals that British troops should be maintained on the Continent on a semi-permanent basis and that they should have joint training arrangements. Schuman was not satisfied with these proposals and demanded a formal treaty with the EDC promising mutual aid in the face of aggression. Eden hesitated but when Secretary of State Acheson came to London on 13 February, they agreed to issue a joint declaration guaranteeing support for the EDC in the event of a threat to any of its members. Schuman was still unsatisfied and finally Eden agreed to Britain's signing a formal mutual defence pact with the EDC to be in force as long as Britain remained a member of NATO. With this formal British commitment the EDC treaty was subsequently signed in Paris on 27 May 1952. The next hurdle which needed to be surmounted was ratification by each of the national parliaments.

It has been frequently argued that, had Britain been willing to join the EDC as a full member, the French National Assembly would have readily ratified the Treaty instead of rejecting it. This can be discounted. The Pleven Plan, as the distinguished French commentator, Raymond Aron, pointed out, led to the most traumatic ideological quarrel in French society since the Dreyfus affair. It was a quarrel, moreover, "whose most apparent issue was German rearmament, but whose deepest significance affected the very principle of French existence, the national state".

At root therefore French objections to the EDC were of the same fundamentalist character as those of Britain, namely that it was likely to supplant the organic traditions of the nation state with those of a supranational bureaucracy or, alternatively, an intergovernmental structure incapable of reacting to an emergency threat. In the case of Britain these fears have persisted largely unresolved up until the present day. But despite the fact that the EDC was an entirely French conception it is quite plain that the EDC aroused more hostility in France than in Britain, if only because where Britain could not seriously entertain becoming a member, France was deeply divided on the proposals. For almost two years after the EDC Treaty had been signed the French Assembly proposed one amendment after another in an effort to pare down its provisions. The other EDC countries were adamant in rejecting any French attempt to emasculate the EDC. Churchill and Eden both sensed by this time that the EDC was doomed and, on a visit to Washington in June 1954, agreed with the Eisenhower Administration that West Germany must be left free to form her own alliances irrespective of the fate of the EDC. By the end of August the EDC had been killed stone dead by the French National Assembly. Since it was not unexpected, and had in fact long been anticipated by Eden, the British Government was not slow in proposing alternatives.

Eden's chief immediate objective at this point was to bring Germany into the NATO alliance with safeguards sufficient to allay French fears, yet without offending German national pride too much. Dr Adenaur accepted Eden's general aims to the point of agreeing to German force limits on a voluntary basis. In the knowledge that the Germans were likely to support his general aims, on their behalf Eden embarked on his mission of diplomacy by proposing a nine-power conference in London comprised of the six EDC countries plus Britain, the United States and Canada, to be held in mid-September. Later he could put whatever agreement was reached to the full NATO Council.

The means Eden conceived of bringing Germany into the western defence system, and through that system into the comity of the western world and the West European integration movement, was the Brussels Treaty of 1946. By bringing both Germany and Italy into this early postwar mutual defence arrangement Eden foresaw a new, just and flexible framework for the construction of the new Western European grouping, with the great built-in merit that it did not discriminate against Germany. Of equal, if not greater, importance : since his concept lacked any supranational elements, Britain could become a full member. Eden rapidly toured the EDC capitals to enlist support for "Western European Union", first Brussels, then Bonn, Rome and finally Paris where he had always known the real difficulties lay. Meanwhile the situation was complicated by a surprise visit to Bonn by Secretary of State Dulles on the day Eden arrived in Paris. Dulles later flew to London, ostentatiously snubbing Paris. Dulles adopted the traditional State Department attitude of the postwar period that nothing but a supranational form of union would satisfy the US Government (for reasons elaborated in the chapter on the Anglo-American Connection).

When Eden visited Paris to meet the French Prime Minister, Pierre Mendès-France, he found him concerned to create strong visible safeguards to calm French fears of German rearmament. French opinion had also been alienated by the Dulles visit to Bonn which in the circumstances suggested that the US Government was backing Germany's wish to rearm against France's profound fear of a militarist Germany. In London, Dulles told Eden that the US Congress had been sold on and was now deeply committed to the EDC or some similar substitute as a means of uniting Europe. Without the EDC or some supranational means towards West European union, Dulles argued, there would "inevitably be" a reduction in US troops in Europe. Dulles was nevertheless persuaded to attend the nine-power conference and to support the Eden plan if the other countries adopted it.

Eden's diplomatic goal was thus threefold. First, to restore German sovereignty and admission to NATO; second, to reassure the French that adequate safeguards could be provided against a restoration of German power; thirdly, to induce the US Government to maintain its troops in Europe without any

supranational political framework for West European union
such as the EDC seemed to provide. The only factor which
could help reconcile these conflicting objectives, Eden felt, was
a new and far-reaching commitment to maintain British forces
on the Continent on a semi-permanent basis. As Eden saw it,
not only was the conference about reconciling Franco-German
interests, but also maintaining the Atlantic alliance intact. His
gamble was to succeed. The Western European Union came into
existence. In Eden's eyes its great advantage over the EDC,
apart from the mere fact of its acceptability to the United States,
Britain, Germany and France—representing those with the most
substantial interests at stake—was that it brought Germany into
the western alliance, and provided a form of European unity
without creating a top-heavy political superstructure, more
especially of a federal character. On 20 October, the WEU was
created and the agreements signed in Paris, thereafter known as
the Paris Agreements. Ratification by all the signatory states
followed, though in the case of the French not without some
hesitation.

It has been said frequently that the greatest achievement of
the EEC (i.e. the Six) was to reconcile France and Germany.
That may be so, but it is also arguable that the creation of the
WEU was a much more fundamental and significant step in
the reconciliation between the two central powers of Western
Europe than the Schuman Plan or the EEC that ultimately
derived from it. It is also often repeated that Britain missed a
unique opportunity to enter the EEC at its very beginning when
it refused to participate in the EDC. Apart from the inherent
dangers of its structure, its unacceptability to France as much as
to Britain, there is no evidence that either British political party
of the time could have persuaded Parliament, still less the British
people, that it was in the British interest to join the EDC and
thus the EEC at its inception.

Among the most striking evidence of the consensus of opinion
which prevailed in the House of Commons even two years after
the EDC had been rejected by the French National Assembly
was the Adjournment debate on European Trade Policy of
26 November 1956 (*Hansard* 1956–7, Fifth Series, vol. 561).
During the debate there was virtual unanimity on the fact that
Britain could not entertain the idea of joining a customs union.
Thus both the leading Conservative Europeanist of the time
Harold Macmillan, then Chancellor of the Exchequer, soon to be

Prime Minister, and Roy Jenkins, soon to be the leading Europeanist on the Labour benches, made categorical statements to this effect in the following terms.

According to Macmillan: "I do not believe that this House would ever agree to our entering arrangements which, as a matter of principle, would prevent our treating the great range of imports from the Commonwealth at least as favourably as those from the European countries. So this objection, even if there were no other, would be quite fatal to any proposal that the UK should seek to take part in a European common market by joining a customs union. I think that we are all agreed there. I feel sure that the Governments of the countries who are negotiating this customs union in Brussels understand and appreciate our position in this matter. So that is out."

This view was unreservedly endorsed by Roy Jenkins in the following terms: "I agree with the Chancellor that it is impossible for us to contemplate going into a full customs union. To do so would mean not only whittling down Imperial Preferences but introducing anti-Imperial Preference. That is a position manifestly impossible to any British Government." These quotations reflect the prevailing opinion on both sides of the House for the next four years if *Hansard* is to be taken at face value. Beneath the surface public pronouncements a great deal of heart-searching was going on as to Britain's postwar role and national identity. The fall of Eden in the Suez debacle precipitated the whole question of Britain's capacity to play an independent role in the most acute form; it also removed from power the most skilled of twentieth-century British diplomatists in the European theatre. Though Macmillan, who succeeded Eden at No. 10 Downing Street, possessed many outstanding political gifts, he had nothing with which to match Eden's vast experience in European affairs. In consequence, during the next seven years the primary initiation of British foreign policy gradually passed from the hands of the Prime Minister and Foreign Secretary into those of the top officials of the Foreign Office working in close collaboration with the US State Department and the Quai D'Orsai, as the chapter on the Civil Service will vividly illustrate.

For the moment, in the wake of Suez, Britain and her continental allies drifted apart. More than ever dependent on American support and goodwill, Britain steadily strengthened her transatlantic ties. By contrast, the search to create a supranational superstructure for the new Western European customs union was daily widening the gulf between the British and the Continental powers. To illustrate this : within a week of refusing to participate in the six-nation Euratom, which included a supranational council to co-ordinate the use of atomic resources, the British encouraged the OECD to push ahead with proposals for a seventeen-nation Nuclear Energy Agency, without any supranational features. The same pattern was to be repeated in 1974 with the OECD's creation of the Energy Action Group which was seen as a more flexible forum for co-operation than the more formalized EEC and UN institutions.

There is little doubt that after the Suez fiasco Macmillan was anxious to hammer out a successful European policy for Britain. However, the 1957-8 negotiations with the Six only confirmed that Britain was primarily interested in free trade, the Six in some form of European unity. Indeed, according to de Gaulle, not only did Britain firmly decline to participate in drafting the Rome Treaty but Macmillan asked de Gaulle in June 1958 to give up the idea of the Common Market for some other alternative. Until 1958 Britain had in fact been pressing for a seventeen-nation free trade area without any external tariff. When in November 1958 this was defeated, Britain established the European Free Trade Area (comprising Britain, Norway, Denmark, Austria, Switzerland, Sweden and Portugal) and called for the closest collaboration with the Six. Not surprisingly, supporters of Britain joining the Six argued that this was the seventeen-nation free trade area in a new guise. In a sense they were right but it was as much a means of practical co-operation in Western Europe as the EEC. Indeed, judging by the lack of progress beyond a customs union among the Common Market countries after 1968 it was a more realistic approach to European co-operation than the more ambitious structures of the Treaty of Rome. Again according to de Gaulle, Macmillan told him in April 1960 that British entry was "unthinkable". A year later Macmillan was fully committed to entry.

If one traces the history of the Conservative Party in the twentieth century up to the mid-1950s it would seem the very least likely candidate to spearhead Britain's entry into the Common Market. Not only had it been nurtured on governing a nation which was a world power in the sense that it was capable of playing a worldwide political, commercial and military role, but it was a party whose whole ethos was based on traditional patriotism. If Labour's appeal was based on the solidarity of the working class and its sympathizers, then the Conservatives had traditionally appealed to "the national interest". There seemed on the evidence then available little possibility of persuading a political party with such a traditional nationalist background to adopt a foreign policy which explicitly concentrated on Europe and involved an appeal to supra-nationality, i.e. a European rather than a British consciousness. In a word, Conservatives were being asked to become Utopian internationalists, which was difficult for a party who have been nationalists since the days of Disraeli. If such a complete reversal of traditional Conservative policy, not to say attitudes, were to be successfully achieved it would take a very long time—unless the conversion campaign was concentrated not on the party as a whole but on the decision-takers and opinion-formers. In fact that is precisely how it seems to have been conducted. But even a selectively concentrated campaign of this kind would probably have proved fruitless except for one major essential precondition —namely that the British political Establishment in the Con-servative party had broadly lost confidence in Britain's ability to solve her national problems. This particular consciousness can be dated fairly precisely to 1956–7. However, before doing so it is useful to go back even further in order to trace the thinking of the Conservative party leaders.

The concept of European unity is not new and has been the subject of debate and discussion on the Continent for several centuries. The contemporary European movement began to gather momentum in Britain following World War II for much the same reasons as it arose on the Continent : to create the kind of continental system which would make the nationalist conflicts of 1914 and 1940 impossible. Parallel to these political move-ments there eventually grew up a host of theories of European integration ranging from the cautious functionalists to the more ambitious federalists to be followed in time by the neo-function-alist and transactional schools. But even before these theories came into circulation the ideas of Continental thinkers began to spread across the Channel. The general aspiration of European governments to achieve greater collaboration was shared, as we have already seen, by the postwar leadership of the Conservative Party including both Winston Churchill and Anthony Eden.

When Churchill became Prime Minister in 1951, however, he

did not lend his support to the movement for Continental union. Indeed, it is alleged that he badly let down the cause which he had in opposition enthusiastically espoused. This is not only a superficial judgment; it is factually inaccurate. Churchill never envisaged Britain becoming a member of a supranational European organization which would effectively supersede the sovereignty of Parliament. It is not even credible on his particular record that he would contemplate such a development, even in the remote future. Common citizenship he might magnanimously propose in the dark hours of the war to the French people but it entailed no surrender of British sovereignty of any sort. On the contrary, his famous "three circles" doctrine of British foreign policy explicitly excluded such a possibility. In this doctrine he advocated that Britain should regard herself as a European power, an Atlantic power, and a Commonwealth power—belonging to all three connections, but belonging exclusively to none of them. Despite appearances, this was not an overextended policy but an accurate description of British spheres of interest at the time. The scale of Britain's commitment was wide open for reassessment according to the circumstances prevailing in each circle of influence at the time. There was plenty of political, strategic, commercial and diplomatic evidence of British interests existing in each sphere in the 1950s even though the military component was declining rapidly.

Churchill's postwar cabinet, however, soon showed signs of dissent. Several ministers, among them Harold Macmillan, then Housing Minister, favoured a major initiative which would enable Britain to take the lead in Europe. After his experiences in the trenches of the Great War and his first-hand observations of the Depression it was not unnatural that Macmillan favoured British participation in the recreation of a new, united Europe. It has been widely put about that had Britain, and specifically the Churchill and Eden Administrations, seized their opportunities, the leadership of Europe was theirs for the taking at any time up to the signing of the Treaty of Rome in 1957. It is really no more than a legend. Leadership on Britain's "own terms" meant a form of Europeanism devoid of supranationalist content and would have simply meant an industrial free trade area and co-operation in defence (already taking place in NATO). But the early Continental Europeans were after something entirely different and would have regarded such a form of unity as not worth striving for with any great effort.

What then made the Conservative Party swing from a world-wide to a European destiny? Basically the answer seems to be because of a loss of confidence in themselves so that they came to look at Britain in much the same way as the continental Europeans looked at Europe in the aftermath of World War II. Changes of this magnitude do not take place overnight. But it took a single event to crystalize that feeling and bring it to a head. One former Conservative MP has said that at Suez the nation (he meant the Conservative Party) suffered a nervous breakdown. It was a classic confrontation between a weak state and a world power, in which the Conservative Prime Minister was toppled ignominiously from office in the wake of an almost unendurable defeat in the eyes of the whole world. The question arose : could a nation that had suffered such a defeat still lay claim to call itself a great power? The theme of the greatness of Britain is an article of faith for Conservative leaders, a tradition maintained in the speeches of Edward Heath as Prime Minister. Perhaps, significantly Sir Christopher Soames has carried over this attitude towards the greatness of Britain into the idea of the greatness of Europe (see *The Times*, 13 October 1973). One suspects that any man or woman who wishes to win the leadership of the Conservative Party in the open field must embrace some view of the greatness of Britain. When in 1956 the current Conservative belief in the greatness of Britain (derived from power and influence as much as any moral authority) was rudely shattered by the economic and political realities, the state of mind of the Conservative Party was wildly confused.

Before describing the first major bid to enter the Community, under the Macmillan Administration, it is worth inserting the recollections of one of the leading protagonists in the entry debate, J. Enoch Powell: "I first registered my lack of enthusiasm for a supranational European framework embracing Britain at the very outset of my Parliamentary career, in June 1950, when together with five other Conservative members I lent my support to the Labour Government in their policy of abstaining from participating in the Schuman Plan (pooling French, German and Benelux coal and steel production). By so doing I forfeited a place in Winston's government when it was formed in 1951. Churchill, of course, provided much of the impetus and inspiration for the immediate postwar collaboration in Western Europe, notably the Council of Europe. But the nature of this collaboration in the future was not closely defined and was allowed to mean different things to different people according to their personal preconceptions. The truth is that Churchill had a generous rather than an analytical frame of mind on this as on many matters of high politics. By contrast Duncan Sandys, for instance, was an unflinching federalist, profoundly committed to the acceptance of the inevitability of the merging of British sovereignty with that of her European neighbours. It must be noted that whatever Churchill may have said, and more important, whatever interpretation was subsequently put upon his words, his government did nothing which could be interpreted as surrendering a shred of British sovereignty to any supranational European political institution. In terms of practical politics he gave absolutely nothing away."

The Macmillan Era
Macmillan had long been one of the "Europeans" of the Conservative Party. As far back as 1939, early in the phoney war in October, he wrote in *Picture Post*: "Many people are asking what kind of Europe one could expect to emerge out of the chaos of today. The picture can only be painted in the broadest colours. But if Western Civilization is to survive we must look forward to an organization, economic, cultural, and perhaps even political, comprising all the countries of Western Europe" (*Tides of Fortune* by Harold Macmillan, Macmillan, 1969). Macmillan became intimately involved in the European Movement in the 1940s and had lamented the absence of a European initiative in the early 1950s. When he came to office in January 1957 his major task was to reassure; indeed, to reassure his political supporters that nothing much had really changed. Instead of grandeur Macmillan presented substitutes, or the illusion of grandeur—better relations with America, a British H-bomb exploded, and a grand tour of the Commonwealth successfully completed. Thanks to the consumer boom initiated in 1958 the Conservatives won their third election victory in 1959 with a majority of 100. At this stage Macmillan had been highly successful—the image of Supermac was very much alive and it gave flesh and blood to Britain and the Conservative Party's own image of itself. His one European foray, with Maudling as his agent, was to head off the EEC by the creation of a free trade area for Europe. However, the French wanted supranational institutions at this stage so it failed. EFTA, however, was created in 1958 and proved within

its own modest ambitions highly successful. After 1959, however, the pressures of reality began to close in, not only on Macmillan and the Conservative Government but on Britain as a nation. For those accustomed to Britain as a leader among the nations the political and economic future looked grim. For those who were unconcerned about Britain's diminishing world role things weren't so noticeably bad. In the background the Civil Service, and especially the Foreign Office was particularly concerned about Britain's role and began to steer its course towards a new European set of goals. By the end of 1960 Macmillan was convinced and set to work to carry his Cabinet and the Conservative Party with him. Considering the importance of the switch it was remarkably easily accomplished—at least within the Cabinet, where only Hailsham, Butler and Maudling among the political heayweights expressed any serious scepticism. There was no violent opposition from within the Cabinet whatsoever. In the Conservative Parliamentary Party opposition was largely confined to the "imperialist" right wing of the party. Though individual members stood against the reversal in policy there were no resignations from the Government. Thus was accomplished a quiet but nonetheless historic revolution in the traditional governing party. With almost no casualties Britain's historic foreign policy was put into reverse. This was achieved, in part, by Macmillan (like Edward Heath some years later) taking the precaution of strengthening the Europeanists in his Cabinet. Thus in the reconstruction of July 1960 he appointed two dedicated pro-Marketeers in the persons of Christopher Soames and Duncan Sandys to the key posts of Agriculture and Commonwealth Relations respectively. During the summer and autumn of 1960, and throughout 1961, a succession of British Ministers met with member governments of the Six. Macmillan himself met with de Gaulle, Adenaur and Fanfani "to test the temperature of the water" as *The Times* put it on 1 March. So far the preparations had been of a preliminary kind with numerous reservations about preserving Britain's historic external relationships outside Europe. The advantages stressed by the government were chiefly economic in the shape of a vastly increased "home market", a faster growth rate, a higher rate of US investment, etc. This marks an interesting contrast to the appeal made to the Six, who essentially came together in the wake of a harrowing defeat because they needed each other. Britain, urged the British government, was to reconnoitre the possibility of membership of the Community on the grounds that it was an obvious economic success. It was still conceived as an enterprise to be undertaken without ditching the United States, the Commonwealth and EFTA. As Harold Macmillan put it to the Commons on 31 July: "If a close relationship between the United Kingdom and the countries of the EEC were to disrupt the longstanding and historic ties between the United Kingdom and the other nations of the Commonwealth the loss would be even greater than the gain." Although Macmillan also went on to argue (4 August), possibly influenced by what he knew of American determination to see Britain "in", that Britain needed to join in order to succeed in the Cold War, the majority of the British people plainly felt their primary allegiances lay elsewhere. In July a poll had shown a large majority in favour of a union with the United States rather than Europe. On 1 August a Gallup Poll showed 38 per cent in favour of entry, 23 per cent against and 39 per cent don't knows. Enthusiasm waned from then on as the likely terms became apparent. At this stage, even in the Cabinet, Maudling, Butler and Hailsham were still dubious about the whole enterprise.

Nevertheless on 2 August Macmillan announced the intention of his Government to "make formal application" for British membership of the European Economic Community in order to discover whether conditions existed in which membership might be possible. It seemed a reasonable proposition and represented on the face of things a cautious approach to an issue which needed to be resolved. The Government gained a Commons majority of 308 for this fairly unexceptionable form of application. It became apparent, however, that the claim to be exploring the possibility of reasonable terms was a cover for an intention to enter the Community on the best terms that were negotiable in Brussels.

Once the decision to apply for entry had been made, it marked the end of several centuries of skilfully maintaining a world network of relationships with no single region favoured at the expense of another. The men who made this decision clearly believed that by "joining Europe" Britain would be able to help create a new and wider power base and thus refurbish the image of Britain as a great power. They were scarcely concerned with economic issues except to sell the package to the various interest groups on whose electoral and financial support they relied. The extraordinary fact remains that the political and economic advantages have never been precisely spelled out either then or at any time since that date (unless one regards the respective White Papers on the EEC prior to entry as genuine prospecti). What the Conservative leadership saw as a political opportunity was in reality merely the opportunity to take place in economic bargaining for a very vague, even dubious political gain. In fact, there was always—and remains—a basic contradiction in Britain joining Europe to remain a great power. For if the Community eventually evolves into an effective political union British citizens will become members of a great power, certainly, but Britain as a nation state with the power to make decisions solely, indeed primarily, in her own interests would by definition have ceased to exist. If on the other hand Britain were to retain her national independence it would automatically exclude Europe from becoming a great power. The choice between national independence and great-power status has yet to be made by Britain or any other member of the EEC. Only the Benelux governments seem completely sold on surrendering national sovereignty, for the obvious reason that they have the most power to gain and the least to lose. The thesis that the British people would exercise greater control over their own destiny as citizens of a super-Europe than as citizens of a middle-rank nation adjacent to a great power was central to the convictions of the Conservative leadership. It is a thesis which is only now being put to the test. So far Britain has demonstrated less rather than more control over her own destiny not only in specific issues such as butter, sugar, VAT etc., but on the broader issues of reducing the scope and size of the CAP; the creation of social and regional funds to compensate Britain for being on the fringe of the Community's growth centres; and, above all, exercising parliamentary control over major issues of any sort. Although it is too early to say reform is impossible, there are few signs of Britain effectively protecting her vital national interests let alone persuading the Community to change any matter of substance. In plain language the vision of Britain remaining a great power through the agency of Europe looks like proving an even greater mirage than the economic opportunity of the vast "home" market of 250 million Europeans (in 1973 Britain ran a deficit with the rest of the EEC in the vicinity of £1,000m. In 1974 it was £2,000m, an entirely non-oil deficit).

In the period 1961–3, Macmillan, Home and Heath, the latter

having been made responsible for "Europe", were extremely guarded in what they said to British audiences : while in Brussels Heath was prepared to make declarations about Britain's commitment to a united Europe—in London there were lofty generalities and evasiveness about details. General de Gaulle was more candid and more precise. In his press conference of 14 January 1963, in which he imposed his first veto, he said :

"The question today is whether they [the British] can accept coming inside a single tariff wall, renouncing all preferences for the Commonwealth, abandoning any privileges for their own farmers, and repudiating the pledges they made to their EFTA partners. This is the real question." The official and majority answer of the Conservative Parliamentary Party by the beginning of 1963 was still yes.

De Gaulle spoke of the British application as a request for membership on its own conditions. He went on : "With British entry into the Common Market it was entirely foreseeable that its cohesion would not hold for long and that in the end there would appear a colossal Atlantic Community under American dependence and leadership which would soon completely swallow up the European Community." It was ironic that on the very same day, 14 January, that the General was holding his twice-yearly news conference, President Kennedy was presenting his State of the Union Address to Congress. Even more ironically, as it transpired, Kennedy told the Congress : "Free Europe is entering into a new phase of its long and brilliant history—moving towards a unity of purpose and power and policy in every sphere of activity." Though Kennedy and De Gaulle may not have managed to get in step, there can be little doubt that Kennedy's support was a crucial factor in the whole of Macmillan's and therefore the Conservative Government's first application. Moreover, though Kennedy himself was to be tragically cut down, the American commitment to British entry remained unwavering right up until its successful accomplishment. Not until America saw the inability of Britain to influence the external relations of the enlarged Community in any significant sense, as America had always envisaged, did that commitment begin to falter.

Meanwhile in 1963 one of the effects of the General's veto was to bring the gut political issues which lay at the heart of the negotiations (although not necessarily the negotiating table), out into the open. De Gaulle never made any secret of the fact that as long as he was President, France should shape Europe as long as she could do so, first to forestall the resurgence of a militarist Germany, and secondly to delay the break out and possible future dominance of what he called the Anglo-Saxons (meaning both the British and the Americans). Thus when Kennedy and Macmillan's hopes were dashed by the January 1963 Elysée press conference De Gaulle was only fulfilling a role which he had long previously determined should take place in one form or another. His distaste for Kennedy's Grand Design was anything but whimsical; now the Grand Design had collapsed at the moment of his choosing.

Macmillan's personal response was predictably virile and in its way more outspoken, though less effective, than the General's. "A great opportunity has been missed and it's no good trying to minimize or disguise that fact," he said on British television. "What has happened in the last few weeks has revealed a fundamental division of purpose. I hate saying it, but France, or at any rate, France's government, is looking backwards. They seem to think that one nation can dominate Europe or perhaps even one man—that's all wrong." The sentiments are understandable from one who had believed in his cause for so long and had probably personally resolved that his government would go in under the best terms it could obtain, but go in anyway. It was because De Gaulle realized just this that his intervention, highlighting the real differences at issue, was so painful. It was as if your opponent at bridge were to seize your hand of cards and lay them for all to see as being vastly inferior to his own, and to do this arbitrarily before the game had actually reached the point when you needed to submit. The Conservative leader was not the only one to smart a little; so did his Cabinet colleagues, the Conservative Party and the nation as a whole (though many were grateful and others admired the General's style). Whether, as Macmillan claimed at the time, De Gaulle's first veto was "bad for us, bad for Europe and bad for the whole free world" is, with the advantage of hindsight, arguable.

What is at this distance in time fairly clear is that De Gaulle saw the "Anglo-Saxons" as one; that if Macmillan saw his collaboration with Kennedy as a natural alliance, De Gaulle saw the British as pawns in a much larger power game in which the Americans were calling the tune. At the time the French press made the rather facile comparison that the British were unable to reach agreement with the Common Market after sixteen months of negotiations while they had concluded a defence pact at Nassau with the Americans in less than three days. There was a certain crude logic in the argument.

Although the General himself made no mention of the Nassau Agreement, or even of Polaris, at his press conference, he later leaked his views informally at a reception for National Assembly deputies. Broadly they ran something like this : "England has turned over to the Americans what atomic forces she had; she could have handed them over to us. Well, she has made her choice. Having turned down my ideas for an Anglo-French or European nuclear deal [at Champs in June and Rambouillet in December] Britain can hardly expect to enter a European political union while leaving her nuclear deterrent under American control until 1980. It is neither a reasonable nor a practical proposition."

The French themselves put forward as their reasons for the veto as (1) Kennedy's offer of Polaris, (2) the Nassau Agreement, (3) the Anglo-Saxon treatment of De Gaulle during the war. The extent to which the nuclear special relationship underlined the survival of the overall "special relationship" in French eyes cannot be overestimated. The American offer of Polaris to the French as an obvious afterthought only rubbed this in, especially since France possessed neither the submarines suitable to launch them nor the thermonuclear warheads to arm them. But it was not only the French who were angered by the Nassau Agreement. It also upset both the West German and Italian governments. Indeed, Adenaur is reported to have regarded De Gaulle's veto as the just riposte to the Anglo-American agreement. Macmillan never really appreciated, at least at the time, the depth of resentment that such a step would provoke. He maintained to the end that "Nassau had nothing to do with the Brussels talks. The negotiations broke down because they were on the point of succeeding." The first point was probably the way Macmillan wished it and so regarded it from his own vantage point. The second is in the nature of a confession. If it is true that they were on the brink of succeeding, then the Macmillan administration was willing to concede a very great deal. The most significant aspect of the De Gaulle veto was that it represented the rejection of America's hegemony every bit as much as the refusal of British entry on the grounds of the incompatibility of Anglo-French economic requirements.

It was inevitable that following De Gaulle's veto there would

. .

be a strong surge of "anti-European" feeling in the Conservative Party, evidenced by such minor displays of petulance as the cancellation of the Royal Visit to Paris and at a deeper level by the almost total absence of anything about Europe in the Conservative Party 1964 election manifesto. The aim of the Conservative leadership soon became clear. Effectively it was to keep faith with their vision of British greatness by pursuing a European course, but to maintain an extremely low profile on their preparations to obtain British entry.

Conservatives Maintain Faith, 1963–70

In spite of the gloomy prognostications of the most ardent "Europeans" (1961–3 vintage) that Britain could not co-operate effectively with Europe unless she joined the EEC, British trade with Western Europe continued to expand while the goal of a united Europe seemed as distant as it had ever been. Yet the faith of the Conservative leadership in their vision of Europe remained unshaken. It seemed the only available role fitting to an ex-imperial power and by its very scope seemed to offer a general panacea to a decently declining world power.

In the period 1963–5, with Macmillan replaced by Douglas-Home, a considerably less committed European, the Conservative Party might conceivably have lost its earlier enthusiasm for the EEC. Bearing in mind that according to Macmillan (speaking on television on 18 September 1973), "We carried the Conservative Party Conference on the Common Market in 1961 more by deference to me and the Conservative leaders than by any great conviction", it seems that this commitment had taken only shallow root in the Conservative Party at large. De Gaulle seems to have read the political situation in Britain as accurately as that in France. He told Macmillan at Rambouillet that Britain, and by that he meant a Britain led by the current Conservative Party, would drastically alter the nature of the Community if she entered at that point. Several days after the announcement of the Nassau Agreement between Macmillan and Kennedy on sharing Polaris missiles de Gaulle took the excuse he was looking for and exercised his veto. All of this was hard for the British to take lying down. It was even more humiliating for the Conservative Party with their visions of British greatness.

It was at this point that the European Commission Information Service astutely realized that this was a make-or-break situation not only for the Conservative Party and its attitudes to the EEC but for the long-term prospects for British entry. Wisely it made great play of the fact (in reality of dubious authenticity in terms of the realities of power both then and now) that the Community's shape and character were determined by the Commission and not the Elysée. This particular campaign was reinforced by the considerable diplomatic talents of Lord Harlech when he returned from Washington. A former Conservative minister with close ties with the Conservative establishment, Harlech had become a convert of Kennedy's vision of a united Europe in which Britain would play a leading, if not the leading role. Another important figure at this period of the maintenance of faith was Sir Eric Roll; he was also profoundly influenced during his period at the Washington Embassy by Kennedy's Atlantic pillars theory. However, as Permanent Secretary of the Department of Economic Affairs (1964–8) his influence was to be felt much more in the Labour Party's attitude to Europe especially through the person of George Brown.

Enoch Powell again takes up the story from his own particular vantage point within the Conservative Party. For the sake of continuity it is worth quoting Mr Powell in full, even if this means going ahead of the narrative so far. "In 1960 when I became Minister of Health, I was not a member of the Cabinet. By October 1961 a British bid to enter the EEC had become the official policy of the Conservative Government. By July 1962, when I became a member of the Cabinet, these issues were for all practical purposes settled. Nevertheless it was known that many industrialists were against entry and the majority of constituency workers were decidedly lukewarm. My own position at this point was to back an entry bid which could further the cause of free trade in Europe, while enabling us to counteract any federalist tendencies in the Community. By January 1963, by which time Mr Macmillan had received the most brutal of rebuffs from General de Gaulle, Iain MacLeod, as party chairman, discussed with me the desirability of Macmillan's resignation in the face of a major foreign policy failure. Personally, I saw then, as I see now, the promotion of trade liberalization as the way in which Britain can participate in Western European co-operation. I am on record as supporting the Maudling concept of European co-operation in free trade without supranational commitment.

"In the light of their previously expressed opposition, the

decision of the Labour leadership in 1966 to explore entry into the EEC represented a complete *volte face*. For myself, when I voted in 1967 to authorize this exploration, it was on the basis of determining what terms were available and in the expectation that the terms available were likely to be unacceptable, not only to us but also to the French, who could be counted upon in the person of the General to say no.

"By 1968 I had become opposed to entry under any terms since it had become apparent that the Community was in the final analysis primarily interested in some form of political unification. By this time, that is the end of the 1960s, I had become clearly aware of the true political character of the EEC and its *dirigiste* approach to economic questions.

"Thus by 1970 I made my opposition to entry into the Community perfectly clear in the election campaign, one of a small minority of candidates to do so—most were careful to say nothing about the EEC at all. In February, March and April of 1971, I made speeches in French, Italian and German in the respective countries to explain why the British people were averse from entry. On 13 September 1971, I made a speech at East Ham in which I stated categorically : 'The first and most important thing to say about British entry is that it is not going to happen.' This was a means of placing myself in a position where I could not back down; it was also a means of giving encouragement to those who opposed entry but were wilting under the barrage of EEC and British Government propaganda. Essentially, however, it was a statement of a permanent belief about Britain and Parliament which I am still confident that history will not refute. Nevertheless when the October vote on entry gained a much bigger majority than I had expected, I believed for a while that I had been handed out a sentence of political death. It must be remembered that the October vote was a vote purely on the White Paper which was on the principle of whether Britain should apply for entry. It is the vote of February 1972 which much more accurately reflected the true margin of support for entry within the Parliamentary ranks. Admittedly a crucial part was played in both votes by the internal political struggles of the Labour Party, though it is a matter of historical fact that it was the support of the Liberal Party which enabled the Government to obtain the legislation, by giving them a majority for the guillotine procedure, without which EEC entry could not have been carried.

"During the course of 1971–2 there was a reaction against entry in the country at large in spite of the massive propaganda campaign being mounted by the Government. In the wake of the vote of 17 February 1972, unparalleled pressure was brought to bear on wavering Conservative MPs. It had quite simply become apparent that without such pressure being applied there could be no majority. In the event the Liberals remained throughout as absolutely essential to the application of the guillotine on the Communities Bill. Moreover it was necessary for the Jenkinsites and the Conservative whips to liaise frequently and secretly in order to guarantee a Government majority.[3]

"During 1973 the commitment of the Labour Party to some form of fundamental renegotiation emerged, and as the Conservative Party became even more deeply committed to economic and political integration in the EEC, nothing was more natural than the Conservative opponents of the EEC, like myself, should find their allies on the other side. This became generally apparent when I participated with Michael Foot on a radio programme on Parliament on 8 June 1973. Foot repudiates as heartily as I do a permanent vehicle for political intervention established in Brussels and subject to the barest minimum of Parliamentary control from Westminster."

The Heath Era
The campaign to maintain support for British entry into the EEC in the Conservative Party won a major battle when Edward Heath was elected to the leadership in 1965. Though Heath drew parliamentary support outside the Conservative "Europeans", almost every Conservative MP associated with the European movement gave him their support. Unsurprisingly Heath soon showed his European commitment in the 1966 Conservative election manifesto and followed it up with the appointment of Russell Lewis from the European Movement to head the Conservative Political Centre. It was no more than an augury of things to come. Heath soon made it clear that there was to be no promotion in the Conservative Party without an unwavering commitment to British entry. It was a requirement he established in opposition and maintained with total ruthless-

[3] Mr Powell confirms the view held and supported elsewhere that unprecedented pressure was put on local constituencies by both the Prime Minister and the Chief Whip to achieve a majority of eight in the decisive vote in February 1972.

ness when he eventually came to power. Nevertheless many Conservative Party activists retained their doubts. These were assiduously wooed by the European Community Information Service (ECIS) with trips to Brussels not only for their own sakes but also to apply pressure from within the Party on recalcitrant MPs.

The character and personality of Edward Health were crucial ingredients in the attitude of the Conservative Party towards the EEC, yet when he was elected in July 1965 he was seen not so much as the champion of Britain's entry into Europe but as a middle-class technocrat and the Conservative answer to Harold Wilson. His main rival, Reginald Maudling, had, it is true, like Heath, been involved in negotiations with the Europeans in 1957–8 (towards a reciprocal free trade area) but he lacked the almost religious belief of Heath that Britain's destiny lay within the EEC. Beginning with his maiden speech in the House of Commons in 1950 when he castigated the Labour Government for refusing to negotiate for British participation in the Schuman Plan, Heath had been bent on British commitment to the supranational institutions emerging on the Continent. Thus, consciously or unconsciously, when the Conservatives elected him as leader in 1965 they had taken their most decisive single step towards entry into the Community. For even if Heath moved from being a Monnet supranationalist in 1950 to a Dahrendorf inter-governmentalist by 1974, he remained utterly resolute in his determination to take Britain in, to the point of staking his entire political career upon it. This being so, it is reasonable to examine Heath's European policy as part of his overall foreign and domestic policies and most of all his monetary and fiscal policies between 1970 and the defeat of his administration in 1974.

In the General Election of June 1970, despite the fact that Heath was to reveal the European issue as the cornerstone of his administration in office, less than 3 per cent of his campaign speeches were devoted to Conservative policy in the Common Market.[4] The Conservative Manifesto was similarly reticent, but included a promise that "Our sole commitment is to negotiate : no more, no less. As the negotiations proceed we will report regularly through Parliament to the country." It also assured its readers that "The opportunities are immense. Economic growth

[4] David Butler and Michael Pinto-Duchinsky, *The British General Election of 1970*, London, 1971, p. 444.

and a higher standard of living would result from having a larger market." Both these promises were highly significant. The first employed the same approach as the previous Labour administration and emphasized the scrutinizing role that Parliament might play. In practice the negotiations were not about the terms of membership as such—they were more or less unconditionally accepted—but about the terms of the transitional period. The second argument, about the expanded home market ensuring higher living standards, was fundamentally fallacious by 1970 since the Kennedy Round tariff reductions had reduced industrial tariffs between Britain and the Six to insignificant levels, evidenced in the growth in trade already taking place (creating a progressively larger imbalance in the Six's favour which was to continue after entry). One of the features of the "enlarged home market" argument for British entry that its proponents and critics alike agreed upon was that to succeed Britain's economy had to be on an upturn of substantial proportions. In other words, a boom had to be engendered prior to British entry.

Thus the creation of a British economic boom was not only a necessary morale booster for Conservative Party supporters of the new administration, it was an absolute prerequisite for Heath's European policy on the grounds advocated. The fact that this vast new home market was not believed in by British industry meant that the necessary investment was never undertaken. But since the government was bent on a boom, the credit was provided and the money supply was increased by an average of very nearly 30 per cent in the first three years of the Heath administration. While the causes of Britain's inflation cannot be divorced from world economic trends such as the steep rise in commodity prices (itself promoted by an earlier inflation sparked by the US Government's refusal to increase taxes to pay for the Vietnam War) the root cause of Britain's internally generated inflation was the Government's own monetary irresponsibility. While the public explanation offered by the Heath Government was that such inflation was permissible if steep rises in unemployment were to be avoided, the importance of maintaining the impetus of growth at the period of entry was almost certainly a cogent if unstated underlying reason. The degree to which the top civil servants stuck to this master plan which they had jointly conceived with the Conservative leader is more clearly apparent in the subsequent chapter on the Civil

Service. Given the degree of commitment the Prime Minister had to the Europeanist cause, none of this should be surprising. There is the further reinforcement that Edward Heath was in many ways more of a bureaucrat and administrator than a politician capable of responding to people's hopes and fears. He was in fact much more in the tradition of the French technocrat, which may help to explain his inability to evoke popular support at home and his much more whole-hearted acceptance by the technocrats in both Brussels and Paris. Some clue to the fact that Heath was both temperamentally and ideologically a technocrat is seen in his proposals in the latter part of his administration to establish an economic policy-making corporatist structure comprising the Government, the CBI and the TUC. No Conservative leader in Britain had previously ever dreamed of denuding the powers of Parliament to such a radical extent in such an undisguised form. Moreover such technocratic tendencies were strengthened by his appointment of such men as Sir Geoffrey Howe as Solicitor-General. While regarding himself as a reformist Howe's deceptively mild manner hid a technocrat of rare determination and technical skill. However, it was no accident that he was to draw up both the Industrial Relations Act and the European Communities Act, the first without consulting the unions until the very last moment and the second with such brevity for such a far-reaching piece of legislation as to suggest his regard for Parliament was not a high one. It may be worth mentioning that not even the French and German Parliaments were as wholly bound to the articles of the Rome Treaty and that neither of them have ever professed to any such high view of their Parliaments as have the British for theirs. It was this degree of insensitivity to the British parliamentary tradition, never mind the popular will, which was to hamper the mobilization of willing converts to the Europeanist cause throughout the life of the Heath administration.

Thus during 1971 the Heath administration ran far ahead of anything that their 1970 election manifesto had suggested they might push through. This was to the consternation not only of the anti-Marketeers but also of those who still felt Parliament worth preserving as the primary democratic forum in which the people could exercise some degree of scrutiny over major legislation and at least minor initiatives on lesser legislation. In the 1970 election no outside observer could have possibly known that the Conservative leadership regarded entry into the EEC as their major policy objective, both foreign and domestic. Among Conservative candidates more than half made no mention of the EEC whatsoever in their election addresses, while of those who mentioned it at all a slight majority expressed themselves against joining. It is clear enough that those who were most strongly in favour saw it as tactically wise to promote entry by stealth on the assumption that most voters were still very much predisposed against. The party leaders encouraged this tactic by taking the position that whether or not it was a good idea to enter the EEC depended on the terms. This may have been tactically sound for all three parties but it hardly allowed the people to have much say in what was the most important constitutional issue since 1910 when the power of the House of Lords was in question. In 1910 a referendum was proposed to solve the question of the Lords' capacity to defeat the Commons' budgetary measures, though an election was eventually fought on the issue.

By contrast, in 1971 suggestions of a referendum were swiftly downed by all three party leaders and the issue was deliberately clouded. Nevertheless, as the Butler and Pinto-Duchinsky study reveals, the remarkable fact is that the Common Market though neglected by the campaigners and media alike, was, after prices, the most common topic of general concern raised on the doorstep. It is a remarkable tribute to the sophistication of the British electorate that they instinctively knew that inflation and Britain's role, either within or outside the EEC, would be the great underlying issues of the early 1970s in Britain. Among the exceptions to this lack of candour about the EEC in the 1970 election were Enoch Powell, who also stressed inflation and immigration (whose interconnection the British public are now beginning to grasp), and the Scottish Nationalists (whose demand for self-government, or at least the forces which lie behind it, is now becoming dimly comprehended). It took another four years before awareness came that the British people, including the people of Northern Ireland, Scotland and Wales, demanded to be consulted over this great constitutional issue and establish the legitimacy of the final decision by a referendum. It was to be a referendum which would inevitably underline the great hunger of the people to be consulted about their political destiny and the fear of those on the Celtic fringes that their revived nationhood was at risk.

Ten days after Edward Heath was swept unexpectedly to

power (very few had predicted a Conservative victory), the British entry negotiations recommenced in Brussels, led by Anthony Barber, perhaps the closest confidant of the new Prime Minister. Some clue to the importance that Heath gave to the issue of British entry (i.e. before any precise terms were known) was the manner in which he rigorously excluded all who were not prepared to give him *carte blanche* on the matter. With the exception of Edward Taylor, who resigned as Under-Secretary of State at the Scottish Office, in opposition to British entry, there were no resignations from the Government from a total of fifty ministers and twenty under-secretaries of state. The very factor which enabled him to carry the Cabinet with him, a total commitment to British entry (to which the British public were in no way privy, and quite unsuspecting of), also provided a kind of retinue of lieutenants who found it difficult to challenge him on other issues. When, like Sir Keith Joseph on economic and monetary policy, they found themselves fundamentally out of step with the Prime Minister, they contented themselves with applying themselves the more intensively to their departmental briefs. By subordinating all other issues to that of European entry the Prime Minister established a degree of momentum that was entirely necessary if entry was to be accomplished. It was, however, built on two fundamental assumptions : that entry under any terms was desirable and that entry once achieved would provide a positive influence on all other policies. Heath held these assumptions with unshakable, almost religious fervour. It was at once the culmination of a dream he had held of Britain joining the postwar European union and the substitute for the sort of family pleasures that might have dulled his crusading ardour. Reginald Maudling for instance, for all his undoubted intellect, skill and experience, was unlikely to have sustained such a vision for so long against such odds. Equally, Maudling would almost certainly have baulked at accepting many aspects of the negotiations with which Heath happily acquiesced, quite apart from Maudling's greater sensitivity to the wishes of the people.

The dispositions within Heath's Cabinet also reflect his determination to push Britain into the EEC as the overriding goal of his administration. On much else he was to change tack under the pressure of events or a change of heart; on Europe there was not even an attempt to tack a little in the face of widespread public hostility, not excluding the ranks of the Conservative Party. Among those who had previously wavered on the Common Market issue, Maudling, in spite of his great experience in trade negotiations in Europe, was assigned the post of Home Secretary; Quintin Hogg was created Lord Chancellor, while Sir Alec Douglas-Home, much more the professional diplomat than the committed politician, was created Foreign Secretary, nominally supremo of the EEC negotiations but in fact largely preoccupied with overall foreign policy. To his closest political allies he entrusted the key negotiating posts : Anthony Barber as Minister for Europe; and to James Prior, formerly Heath's parliamentary private secretary, the key non-Foreign Office portfolio of Agriculture where the greatest amount of negotiating obviously had to be done both before and after entry. They were highly contrasted characters. Barber, the war hero and prisoner-of-war who used his captivity to study for a law degree and who went on to become a successful business man, assumed a breezy, fast-talking, self-confident manner. Prior, the Suffolk farmer who had inherited his land, was slower, more earthy in style, not unlike a friendly uncle. Though, in the tragically premature death of Heath's Chancellor of the Exchequer, Iain MacLeod, Barber was to move to the Chancellorship, he had tasted the atmosphere of the negotiations and took a close interest in them thereafter. Within the Cabinet he was a consistent pusher of entry if only to provide the prospect of the vast new home market that he, Heath and Peter Walker were readily extolling. When Barber left his European negotiating brief Heath made a tactically shrewd appointment. He appointed Geoffrey Rippon, like Barber a barrister, who treated the negotiations like any other brief, as something to expedite to the maximum benefit to his client, in this case Britain. The fact that he might not understand the underlying issues at stake as distinct from the purely technical ones was for Heath's purposes a positive advantage. As Ralf Dahrendorf indiscreetly said when he was still an EEC Commissioner, if the real issues at stake had been placed within the negotiations and made clear to the British people, there is not much doubt that Britain would never have joined.

Meanwhile within the Heath Cabinet an inner group of Ministers was organized to ensure that whatever terms were obtained they would be given parliamentary approval. At a very early stage Heath seems to have decided, no doubt influenced by his own experiences in the preliminary negotiations of the early 1960s, that he would make his main effort at West-minster rather than Brussels. Brussels could only decide so much; in fact it was Pompidou who could unlock the gates, but he demanded what the French had always demanded, an uncon-ditional acceptance of the Community as it stood. The negotia-tions, as the chapter on the Civil Service will underline, were about a package saleable to the EEC constituency. The Six rightly perceived that the only concessions had been on marginal issues mostly coming under the transitional period. Hence the major undertaking for Heath, once the go-ahead signal had been received by the French President (at this point for all practical purposes President of the Six), was the organization of his political forces at home so that the tide of public support for British entry would aid the passage of the EEC Bill through Parliament. Though public support never quite gathered the momentum Heath had hoped for, it did gather ground suffi-ciently by the autumn of 1971 for the Bill to become enacted. This was, however, much more due to Heath's parliamentary and tactical skills than any limited success he might have achieved in gaining public support. Above all it was due to the fixity of purpose of the Prime Minister to pass the necessary legislation however opposed the general public might be and however much divided both the major parties had become over the issue. Essential to this ruthless parliamentary campaign were Lord Carrington (Minister of Defence but also an adept behind-the-scenes parliamentary fixer), Willie Whitelaw, Leader of the House of Commons, Francis Pym, the Chief Whip, and Geoffrey Rippon, the Minister negotiating entry.

As a form of back-up to the official party leadership in Parliament a group of backbenchers known as the Conservative Group in Europe made its services available to the party in the summer of 1970. It had three distinct functional aims: first to promote the campaign for entry in the country, second to pro-mote close relations with Continental political parties, and thirdly, and possibly most significantly, to promote the cause of British entry into the EEC in Parliament. A group of around ten MPs led by Sir Tufton Beamish comprised the spearhead of the Group which in time enlisted the majority of all Conservative MPs. The Group was not without its press and public relations arm which included George Gardiner, then chief political corre-pondent of Thomson Regional Newspapers and later a Conser-vative MP. In the chapter on lobbies we will consider the extent to which various leading Fleet Street commentators, while wearing the cloak of reasoned objectivity, were in fact as actively committed as any elected politician. Above all its other uses the Conservative Group for Europe provided the apparatus which was to be deployed by Norman St John-Stevas to mobilize backbenchers in support of entry.

One of the interesting features of the European issue is that it so strikingly transcended party politics that it offered a rare illustration of the extent to which both major British political parties overlap and the extent to which, in spite of their philosophic presuppositions, they are largely non-ideological coalitions. Thus the anti-Marketeers united the traditionalists in the Tory Party and the Tribune socialists in the Labour Party, both arguably because they retained a vision of political and economic progress that could best be pursued within the national framework. Not least among the national institutions that the anti-Marketeers were seeking to defend was the constitutional supremacy of the British Parliament. It is no accident that the two outstanding Parliamentarians of the 1970s, Enoch Powell on the Right and Michael Foot on the Left, were both prominent among the ranks of the anti-Marketeers. It is equally striking how the leading Marketeers sometimes scarcely concealed their contempt for the Parliamentary tradition. Even *The Times*, no friend to the anti-Marketeers, was moved to point out that Geoffrey Rippon's reports to the House on his discussions with the Six revealed a manner "bordering on the contemptuous ... Mr Rippon's approach seems almost as though he has something to hide". A group of Labour Marketeers, sensitive to the offensiveness of Rippon's high-handed treatment of Parliament, visited Whitelaw and urged a more conciliatory tone if Labour's rebels were to come over to the Government side on the crucial vote.

Throughout the spring of 1971 the battle lines began to be drawn, the pro-Marketeers in the Conservative Group for Europe and the anti-Marketeers in the 1970 Group led by Sir Derek Walker-Smith, a leading QC, and Neil Marten, the Member for Banbury who had declined office under Heath because of his unwillingness to back British entry. Both groups assiduously wooed members, put up questions to Ministers and made sure their viewpoints were expressed on all major party committees. Yet their importance was probably ancillary to the vital questions: when would the vote take place and in what form?

On balance the Government favoured delaying the vote until October for two principal reasons. First, because they needed to consolidate their pro-Market support in the constituencies and secondly because many MPs might react unfavourably to the idea of being rushed into deciding an issue of such historic importance. Among the voices counselling delay on the former grounds was Sir Michael Fraser, the shrewd party manager, and on the latter grounds, Willie Whitelaw, who maintained perhaps the most open lines to backbench feeling of any member of the Heath administration. It was to prove a far-sighted decision and was to provide the essential time that the pro-Marketeers, with their control of the party machine and their far greater financial resources nationally, could the more readily exploit. Certainly in early June the much-maligned opinion polls showed the public generally hostile to entry. On 16 June the Cabinet decided to have a preliminary debate in July but the vote of principle in October. Again Whitelaw must be credited with the more reliable political instincts than either his Prime Minister or the Minister for Europe, both of whom favoured the ready despatch of the issue by holding a full debate in July. If Whitelaw's advice (supported by the Whips) had not been heeded there is a very good chance that the number of Conservative rebels would have been appreciably greater, perhaps fatally so as far as Heath's European policy was concerned. It must be conceded that the Prime Minister was sufficiently impressed by the weight of advice given to him on the dangers of an early vote of principle to restrain his own personal inclinations on the matter.

Meanwhile the pressures were building up within both major parties for a free vote in the autumn debate. In July both anti-Market and pro-Market members of the 1970 Committee of backbenchers recommended a free vote to emphasize that this was a constitutional issue on which Parliament must express a corporate view, not least because it concerned the future power of Parliament. Across the chamber the Labour pro-Marketeers pressed the Prime Minister (privately of course, as "secret" allies) for a free vote in the hope that the Labour whip would also be withdrawn. Had Heath responded to this invitation at this time it is not improbable that the Labour whip would have been withdrawn and then there would have been a free vote in all parties. The possibility of defeat was sufficiently credible at this time for the Prime Minister to turn down the proposal for a free vote at one of his presidential-style press conferences at

Lancaster House. In an off-guarded moment on the same occasion he revealed that "The leaders of the Community expect this Government to use its majority in the Commons to carry it through. This was the only basis that the Six were prepared to negotiate."[5] This was a far cry from the Prime Minister's previous claims that his sole commitment was "to negotiate no more, and no less" and his oft-repeated assurance to MPs that they would be free to make up their own minds. Answering questions, the Prime Minister was emphatic that it was unthinkable to visualize negotiations where the Cabinet, having accepted the terms, would not then command its supporters to vote for acceptance also. The forcefulness of his manner and the strength of his rebuttal of the idea of a free vote ensured that not many Conservative anti-Marketeers were convinced by the argument that once the psychological pressure had been applied for a period (which would serve the dual purpose of weakening the resolve of the prospective Conservative rebels and meanwhile putting the onus on Labour pro-Marketeers to rebel to ensure a majority for the Government) the whips would be lifted at the last moment. Such a move would suggest a belief in the importance of the individual MP hitherto not credited to the Conservative leader. It would also pre-empt the possibility of a Labour free vote since it would suggest a "me-tooism" or merely plain opportunism, a characteristic with which Fleet Street had for so long packaged the Leader of the Opposition even as they had represented the Prime Minister as a man of supreme integrity. Although the suspense of the precise alignments was to last all summer it was the Prime Minister rather than the Opposition leader who was to reveal himself as the supreme tactician.

Within the ranks of both major parties in Parliament there grew up an unofficial whipping system in which the pro and anti factions marshalled support. Since the official policy of the Conservative Party was so firmly turned towards entry, and since the Prime Minister had so clearly staked his whole administration—indeed, with characteristic courage, his entire career—on the success of the negotiations, there was every psychological incentive for the Conservative Group for Europe to enlist supporters. In January 1971 the Group had more than one hundred members, and a further hundred who they believed they could recruit without much trouble; another hundred or more Con-

5 *The Financial Times*, 13 July 1971.

servatives were either agnostic or hostile. By the beginning of May the Group had pulled in about half of those falling into the second category. The next phase involved moving on to the offensive to win converts from among the agnostics in the third category. Seminars were held in Westminster, a score of doubtfuls were taken by St John-Stevas (paid for by the Group) to have lunch with the British Ambassador in Paris, Christopher Soames (of whom only two failed to vote with the leader), and conferences were held with conservative parliamentarians from France and Italy. The whole range of high-level public relations was laid on, down to "select" dinner parties in the Commons, one attended by the Prime Minister. Aside from any ruffled feelings of the Carlton Club at having been upstaged in such traditional Tory means of promoting great parliamentary causes there was a general recognition that such methods should not be despised.

Meanwhile the Conservative anti-Marketeers drew increasing encouragement from the news emerging from Brussels as the negotiations became more and more bogged down. Their numbers included fifteen "gut" anti-Marketeers led by Sir Derek Walker-Smith, Sir Robin Turton and Neil Marten who had from the very early '6os remained staunchly opposed to entry under any conceivable terms. Then there were five Ulster Unionists who were opposed to anything likely to undermine the existence of Ulster. Finally, there were two who had voted in favour of the Labour application, Enoch Powell and John Biffen, but who now saw the Conservative entry bid as a virtually unconditional application which would cast Britain's political and parliamentary sovereignty on to the slag heap of history. The later association of Powell with the Ulster Unionists grew at least in part from this anti-Market alliance with more than a trace of anti-Whitehall overtones. In addition to this hard core group of around twenty-two anti-Marketeers there were about another forty who were opposed for a variety of specific rather than general reasons. According to the "official" Government whips there were a further seventy odd doubtfuls and less than 200 definitely in favour in February; by mid-year, as we have seen, the Conservative Group had made inroads into all but the group of hard case anti-Marketeers. The months of June and July more or less witnessed the turn of the tide within the Conservative Party for the Marketeers. It is ironic that the event which gave the greatest boost to their morale, the Paris summit, was to provide a version of the new Europe which was to turn to dust within two years. It was around this time that Norman St John-Stevas, who had gained considerable experience in unofficial lobbying from his anti-abortion activities, calculated that there would be a maximum of around forty-one defectors against the Government line; three months later there were in fact thirty-nine Conservatives who voted against, two (including Edward du Cann, a former chairman of the party) who abstained and one who was seriously ill and therefore unable to cast his vote in favour. As St John-Stevas was at pains to emphasize, the use of a free vote would probably increase the number of Tory defectors in marginal terms only, whereas in positive terms it would win over public sympathy and more important still make it a great deal easier for the Labour rebels to hold firm. Any decision in favour of a free vote on the Conservative side would need to be announced very late in the day, a piece of advice which the leadership followed to the letter. Curiously, though St John-Stevas thus provided critical support for Heath's major policy bill it was not until the latter part of his administration that he was offered a Government post. Meanwhile, the Conservative anti-Marketeers stood firm at about very nearly forty in August despite the grim assurances from the Government whips that by the time the House reassembled they would have cut this by 50 per cent. The nature of the pressure applied on Conservative MPs, either to stiffen their resolve to vote with the Government or to prevent them from joining the ranks of the anti-Marketeers, encompasses a wide range which needs examining with care since it lies at the heart of the claims made for the role of the individual MP. It needs perhaps to be recorded that on few issues are MPs wooed with such assiduity. Moreover, the issue, which by common assent transcended party politics, also elevated the individual MP to an importance to which he was but rarely accustomed.

The first thing to clear away is that pork-barrel politics, of the kind that are part and parcel of the US Congress, have no real equivalent under the British system. Thus the siting of some industrial project is not conferred to curry favour with an MP but, apart from its intrinsic merits, to curry favour in the constituency with the electorate for the sake of the party. Thus it is in general a reverse process going on. That is, the MP is fundamentally under obligation to prove his loyalty to the party by voting consistently with his party. The implicit reward for such loyalty, combined with some modicum of ability, is office of some sort. In most modern administrations in Britain it needs very nearly a hundred MPs merely to staff the Government benches. Although the Prime Minister has the ultimate say in who should serve in his Cabinet he takes constant advice from his whips on the personal qualities of the members of his party —including their voting records. There is also the small change of party patronage in the shape of delegations abroad and seats on select committees. It is a sad commentary on the weakness of the Commons committee system that apart from the extremely powerful Public Accounts and Expenditure Committee there is no other single Committee which has sufficient prestige to be considered anything but a minor reward for loyalty. The scope for providing the staff and research facilities for such committees is almost unlimited. Their constitutional powers have not yet been fully exercised and it remains chiefly for them to be better financed for them to make a substantial contribution to the parliamentary system. A select committee on foreign affairs, for instance, adequately equipped, could have performed a vital role in the scrutiny of the terms of both Conservative and Labour applications to join the EEC. The final weapon is the armoury of the Government whips in the use of their honours system. It would be churlish not to say libellous, to examine the New Year's Honours system with too fine a toothcomb. That the Government dispensed favours there can be no doubt : it would be surprising, given the existence of the system, and the importance of the issue, had they not done so.

But the real battleground for the pro-Marketeers during 1971 was to be in the constituency. If parties, their policies and leadership (or more cynically the defects of the alternative party's policies and leadership) determine elections rather than the candidate, then it is with such overall policies and leadership that the electors are chiefly concerned. Thus the general antipathy towards the EEC which confronted most Conservative MPs in their constituencies in the summer of 1971 was not their chief concern. Rather was their concern with the attitudes of the local party officers—notably the constituency chairman and the local agent—in whose hands their future adoption lay. While the Conservative Central Office and the Conservative Political Centre set about marshalling support for entry in the early summer, their efforts, at least to begin with, fell on stony ground. But when the Prime Minister addressed the Conservative

Central Council on 14 July at the Central Hall, Westminster, packed with constituency workers, the tide began to ebb in favour of the Marketeers. The anti-Marketeers afterwards referred to this meeting as the "Nuremberg Rally".

The remaining key group who had to be won over were the 400-plus Conservative party agents. Since the party was their paymaster there wasn't much doubt that they would, for the most part, co-operate with Central Office. But the leadership wanted more than that: it wanted and eventually won their active support in bringing round the local associations, who right up until the spring of 1971 had been strongly opposed despite ten years of pro-Europeanist propaganda seeping down from the party hierarchy. The swing may perhaps be largely explicable in the proverbial deluge of literature that descended on the constituencies from the European Movement, the EEC Information Office and the Government, who supplied the Conservative Party with something not far short of a million copies of the White Paper, free. To such a barrage the anti-Marketeers had no response, lacking both the organization and financial resources which had always been at the call of the Marketeers.

There were pressures in the constituencies on Conservative members of both pro and anti sympathies, though understandably, given the fact that the party machine, both at the centre and at the constituency level had swung in favour, the pressures on the antis were far greater. Among the best known was the pressure applied by the Banbury constituency organization on Neil Marten. On 14 July the agent and constituency chairman saw the then national Party Chairman, Peter Thomas; the constituency executive called a meeting on 12 August to discuss Marten's meetings on the Common Market; on 11 August Marten was presented with an emergency resolution expressing support for a three line whip (in total support) on the Common Market. In Woodstock town hall on 12 August, Marten defended himself in public, reminding his audience that he had stated openly in his election address that he was opposed to entry and shrewdly pointing out that the Prime Minister had himself said (less than a month before) that the issue was "above party politics". The meeting nevertheless passed the resolution by 49 votes to 10.

The Conservative leader was confidently informed by late September that the party had swung behind him, both at the constituency as well as the parliamentary level. Thus he approached the annual party conference in Brighton in the first half of October with complete confidence that the vast majority of the party had been won over. As happened with the Labour Party, the conference organizers arranged the Common Market debate to be held on the very first day, an undisguised attempt to defuse the issue, and also as with the Labour Party, to head off whatever anti-Market groundswell arose. Within the space of three hours the Conservative Party disposed of the issue by an overwhelming vote of 8 to 1 in favour of the motion. "This conference welcomes the successful outcome of the negotiations to join the EEC and urges full support for British entry." Something like seventy motions had expressed unqualified support and only four outright hostility. The day was too one-sided to fit the description of a "great debate".

Among the ranks of the big battalions in favour of entry, there was a spirit of exhultation—a spirit more akin to the people of an emergent country on the brink of independence, such was the intoxication of the Paris summit and the prospect of a comfortable parliamentary victory ahead. Geoffrey Rippon spoke in breezy terms that the Six feared that "the armoured brigade of our language, our technology and our way of life would be thrusting across Europe once Britain had joined"; while Norman St John-Stevas conjured up visions not just of another all-conquering Normandy landing (like Rippon) but of the Queen as a potential Empress of Europe. And the last word was had by the perennial darling of Conservative conferences, Sir Alec Douglas-Home, who saw no future for Britain's youth except in a united Europe. By contrast the views of the anti-Marketeers were few. Sir Derek Walker-Smith, largely concerned with the economic balance sheet, told the delegates that on the evidence the costs were certain, the benefits unproven. Finally, Enoch Powell, the man who must be considered the only major Conservative politician who could effectively articulate the fear of millions of anti-Marketeers who had voted Conservative, reading from a prepared statement, tremulous with the solemnity of the occasion, warned of the long-term political consequences. He ended : "I do not believe this nation, which has maintained and defended its independence for a thousand years, will now submit to see it merged or lost; nor did I become a member of our sovereign parliament in order to consent to that sovereignty being abated or transferred. Come what may, I cannot and I will not . . ."

II

THE LABOUR PARTY

UNLIKE THE CONSERVATIVE Party, whose history
for the last one hundred years would lead one to expect it to
espouse the national rather than the international cause, the
Labour Party would appear to be much more orientated towards
an internationalist ethos. Yet if the attitudes of Ernest Bevin,
by general consent the greatest of Britain's Labour Foreign
Secretaries, is anything to go by, Labour's internationalism was
rooted in the principle of securing the interest of the British
people first and foremost and then seeking to improve the general
overseas climate of events. It was no more than a transference
to the international sphere of the tactics of British trade unionism
in which Bevin had been nurtured and subsequently learnt to
lead. As there was no such thing as a national interest which
did not first take account of the interests of the union you had
been elected to represent, so Bevin never lost touch with the
reality that foreign policy began and ended with British national
interests and that any international arrangements were bound
to endure only in so far as they paid due attention to those
national interests. The fact that the nation state was still the
primary focus of people's loyalties throughout the world, including Western Europe, was incontrovertible to most members of
the Labour Party, however lustily they might sing the Inter-
nationale at party conferences. Thus, weary of even the memory
of involvement on a continent that for nearly six years had
sapped Britain's vitality, exhausted its treasure worldwide, thus
helping to dissolve its empire, and, above all, drained its blood
and those of its extra-European allies, the Labour Party was in
1944 generally and understandably hostile to any intimate
involvement of Britain in a politically supranational context.
It came as no surprise to anyone, therefore, that when in 1945
the French socialist party held a conference of West European
socialists, the British Labour Party found itself, in the person
of Denis Healey (who was then the International Secretary of
the Party), out of step with all the other socialist parties present.

Nevertheless, because the British Labour Party was the only party present actually in power, France's Léon Blum had no hesitation in asking Healey to draft the conference resolutions. Hugh Dalton, Minister of Economic Affairs, who was chairman of the International Committee at this time, said candidly : "We are interested in power and policies which can command sufficient public and parliamentary support to be enacted into legislation." By implication, the continental socialists were very much enamoured of idealist resolutions which had little hope of enactment. Sometimes in this period the British socialists found they had allies among the Scandinavians but mostly it was quite simply Britain v. the Rest.

At the Congress of the Hague, Ernest Bevin as Foreign Secretary was present at the head of a small British party of official observers. The Congress consisted predominantly of federalists. Many ex-Prime Ministers and ex-Foreign Ministers were present, of whom Churchill was the most illustrious. Coinciding with the Congress, Denis Healey gave a lead to thinking in the Labour Party on the issue by writing *European Union,* which discussed the problems of federalism with considerable realism. At the same time Dalton, who was the current chairman of the International Socialist Committee, had the power of the Committee substantially reduced. His reasoning seems to have been that German power should be permanently curbed and that to create a weak and at the same time overly ambitious supranational framework would simply play into Germany's proven national susceptibilities, at least in the long-term future when German power and pre-eminence in Europe would be restored.

By the time the Council of Europe first met, Herbert Morrison had succeeded Ernest Bevin as Foreign Secretary and leader of the British delegation. According to William Pickles, "He was a likeable chap but he was the worst Foreign Secretary Britain had possessed for some time, imbued as he was with the vaguest kind of woolly internationalism." Morrison was in fact strongly opposed to Pickles' anti-federalist line. What is interesting, in the light of subsequent talk of co-operation between the social democratic parties of Western Europe, is that from the beginning of the Council of Europe a Socialist group of delegates met on an informal basis. They soon discovered that sharing socialist principles was one thing, but sharing concepts of the role of parliament and the fundamentals of democracy was quite another —the gulf was enormous and unbridgable.

At the Council of Europe the Tories produced a resolution in favour of the Schuman Plan drafted by David Maxwell-Fyffe, signed by everyone in the Conservative delegation except Churchill himself (Eden, who was most certainly opposed, was absent). As any member of the Conservative Party could have told the Council of Europe, anything that does not bear the signature of the leader of the Conservative Party, whether in or out of office, is not worth anything. Harold Macmillan, asked why he was running with so many woolly federalists, replied to the effect that "we can only work with what we find".

According to Pickles again : "The truth is that there is a fundamental difference here in approach between Continental pragmatism, which consists of making the facts fit the treaty and the wording of particular resolutions, and British pragmatism, which believes in acting more or less pragmatically first, then putting down the essence or the principle derived from what has already been done." It is a difference enshrined in the dissimilarities between the Code Napoléon and the practice of the Common Law, the difference between a centralized, bureaucratic state and that of a slowly evolved parliamentary system and relatively decentralized democracy.

Meanwhile in 1951 Churchill came to power once more. As we described in the previous chapter there was considerable disappointment on the Continent that his intentions on the score of British commitment to a supranational form of European co-operation were much more modest than they had led themselves to believe. The history of the Schuman Plan, or the Coal and Steel Community as it became, the chief forerunner of the EEC, illustrates the conflict between theory and practice which was to mark the progress of Western European attempts at unification during the next quarter of a century.

From 1951 to 1957 the Coal and Steel Community worked very well. It was a success story at a time when there was an overall surplus of steel. But when forecasting began to go awry and a pronounced shortage of steel arose the outlook became noticeably less rosy. As long as Jean Monnet ran the Coal and Steel High Authority himself things ran reasonably well. His invariable method was to talk to the governments concerned before attempting to draw up any regulations, thus ensuring both their consent and co-operation and sometimes their critical advice to drop the proposed regulations forthwith. His successor em-

ployed a more distant, more formal and ultimately less successful approach.

The European Defence Community, unlike the Coal and Steel
Community, never got off the ground at all, yet, according to
Lord John Hope, it was around for years being discussed. As
Lord George Brown admits, the EDC in the end actually held
up military co-operation. However, of greater interest to our
theme, and certainly much less well known, is the extraordinary
draft treaty or Statute of the EPC, the European Political Community. In those early days of debate about the nature of a
future European Community the British employed the word
"functionalist" as their means of approach when they really
meant pragmatist, creating misunderstanding from then until
now. Functionalism, however, was not the only principle which
prevailed in this embryonic period for the EEC.

The striking flaw in the EPC draft treaty was that it handed
over to a high authority in articles 35 and 36 the right of decision
over (a) expenditure over arms and (b) the setting of defence
manpower requirements. In effect, taken together, these clauses
gave the high authority the right of decision in issues of war
and peace. Moreover, the only check on the executive of the
EDC was the emergent and deeply divided European Parliament. There was no Council of Ministers in the original Monnet
Plan to represent the direct interests of the nation states of
Western Europe who might eventually join. It is therefore no
small wonder that the original Coal and Steel Community
member states threw out both the EPC and the EDC as danger-
ous exercises in bureaucratic empire-building. All these develop-
ments, with their minimalist approach to democratic checks and
balances, only tended to confirm the British Labour Party's
distaste for the embryonic community which was beginning to
coalesce. Nevertheless, from such unlikely beginnings an *ad hoc*
committee was set up comprising representatives from both the
Council of Europe and the Coal and Steel Community. This
committee then went on to produce a report which it subsequently presented to the Coal and Steel Community High
Authority at a meeting at Messina in 1957 which was to mark
the emergence of the EEC itself.

If the Labour Party stood aloof from the gestation period of
the EEC, the Foreign Office was quite Olympian in its detach-
ment and commitment not to become involved in any European
"entanglement". This lasted for a decade after the cessation of

the war. However, when Sir Frank Lee became the Permanent Under Secretary at the Treasury, the Continentalists gained one of their most effective champions. For Sir Frank emerged as not only a persistent, but a greatly persuasive, champion of British commitment to the new Community coming into being. Indeed his role went further than a generalized form of lobbying. According to Lionel Robbins, later Lord Robbins, it was Sir Frank Lee who finally converted Harold Macmillan to stake his political fortune upon British entry into the EEC. The departure of Anthony Eden (always a staunch sceptic of the value of Britain belonging to a supranational community) from Downing Street in 1957, gave Lee the kind of scope he needed to plant the seeds of a radical new commitment. As we shall see in greater detail in the chapter on the Civil Service, the years 1957 to 1961 saw the gradual conversion of the Treasury to entry, though the kind of support they received was, to say the least, of a dubious quality. A survey of economists revealed that a majority were in favour, but, as Lionel Robbins candidly admitted, it was not on economic grounds, about which nothing could be predicted with any certainty, but on broad general grounds of a more creative internationalist role for Britain to play once more, this time in Western Europe. He believed at the time that Britain could dominate the infant EEC once it entered its chief councils. It is worth noting that the chief ideologue of the post-war Conservative Party, Rab Butler, and the one who most nearly corresponded with the Right-wing of the Labour Party, was still hostile to the embryo Community. Macmillan, with a political astuteness which helped to create the legend of Super-mac, shrewdly brought him into the negotiations thereby making a convert of him on the grounds that "we can't keep chopping around". With professionally committed civil servants at his elbow, his commitment, as with all Ministers subsequently involved in the negotiations (Peter Shore excepted), progressively increased. No such method was available to Labour to help the dissenters to step into line behind the party leader.

Indeed, up until 1961, the Labour Party had not felt it necessary to adopt a closely defined corporate view of Britain's relations with the Common Market. While various MPs were undoubtedly firmly committed, their views seemed to have very little effect on the various cliques to which members of the party belonged. Such leading members of pro-European organizations as Alfred Robens, Kenneth Younger and Roy Jenkins found themselves allied to Douglas Jay in defence of Hugh Gaitskell, who at no stage held any great enthusiasm for European political commitments. There is more than a mere suggestion at this point that the Labour Party would have preferred to remain corporately indifferent to Europe. Macmillan's decision to apply for entry, however, demanded a response from the main opposition party.

In 1961 the Labour Party was still deeply divided over Hugh Gaitskell's leadership. The Party Conference of that year had been a victory for the Gaitskellites after their reverse of the previous year. Gaitskell's position was nonetheless far from secure. Harold Wilson, not yet heir apparent, was making speeches which could be regarded as neutral, though by August (1962) the *Guardian* observed that he had read his Pickles, meaning he had become critical of entry. Certain events at this time probably helped to strengthen his resolve to stay out.

In July 1962, Gaitskell attended the Socialist International where he was bitterly attacked by Belgium's Foreign Minister Henri Spaak (whose daughter later married Sir Michael Palliser, British Ambassador to the EEC) for being cool towards the emerging EEC. Later the same month he attended a Commonwealth Socialist conference where they were by contrast friendly and understanding towards him, though still commending the Commonwealth and worldwide interests of Britain. In the background Gaitskell's chief political adviser had been William Pickles, then a lecturer at the London School of Economics. Around this time Pickles relates that Gaitskell avoided him. "No doubt," Pickles adds, "to make up his mind for himself." Pickles provided Gaitskell with a paper critically assessing the prospects, which was then sent on by him to (later Sir) Frank Soskice inviting a reply in favour of entry. As Pickles relates, "When I later met Gaitskell at the Grand in Brighton he told me he was going to be tough." He was. He made the speech reminding his listeners of the 1,000 years of British independence which could not lightly be surrendered. Meanwhile Harold Wilson was still making speeches which could be described as neutral.

Almost certainly to his own surprise and considerable relief, Gaitskell found that his attitudes and assessment of the Common Market were popular with most of his opponents within the party. Moreover his Market views only antagonized a relatively small minority of his former supporters. Thus it was that by

1962 the Labour Party found itself effectively opposed to British entry. Its precise position was to support entry on terms that had been proved unacceptable to the Six even in 1958. Such a position was predictable given that the Conservative Party was advocating entry, and opposition of this particular sort provided a means of uniting the pro and anti factions in the party. The posture adopted by the party in 1973, that is to renegotiate entry according to specified terms, served very much the same purpose though possibly with far greater justification given the generally adverse effects of the terms of entry.

Not long after the 1962 Labour Party Conference the European issue became once more an apparently academic question as the talks collapsed in the wake of De Gaulle's veto. The Labour Party was spared for the moment the need to think out the implications of EEC entry and its own attitude to those implications. This was in fact to prove a great disadvantage to the stimulation of any effective public debate at a later stage. Hugh Gaitskell's death also removed a fixed point around which the internal debate within the party might have revolved. Nevertheless the victory of Harold Wilson seemed to indicate that Gaitskell's attitude to Europe would be maintained, especially since his victory had been achieved over the leading pro-European, George Brown. That Wilson genuinely believed that British food prices and the Commonwealth connection would be harmed there can be little doubt. The fact that George Brown became deputy leader of the party was also to have great significance for the future course of events.

CDS, 1961–64

The Market seemed a dead issue at this point. The Campaign for Democratic Socialism (CDS), founded originally by Hugh Gaitskell to fight against CND, the Campaign for Nuclear Disarmament, did not however drop the issue. Its most active workers included the keenest Labour "Europeans", led by Bill Rodgers and Dick Taverne. Tony Crosland, Roy Jenkins and, in its early days, Douglas Jay, were all members. Its original aims were to campaign in all sections of the party in favour of Gaitskell's policies. It is not clear to what extent CDS was finally responsible for Gaitskell's success in 1961. What is certain is that CDS made a large number of converts among the more ambitious young moderates in the Labour Party. Much of this success grew out of a university network which was especially strong at Oxford and Glasgow.

When CND waned, CDS not unnaturally looked around for new fields to conquer. Douglas Jay's rapid disassociation from CDS indicated that it had chosen Europe as its target. CDS in fact officially wound itself up even before the 1964 election, but by then the network of well-placed bright young men was established throughout the party. The watchword of Europe was the galvanizing force for the crusade which followed. It also drew extensively on a well-established set of connections with the Continent.

CDS had never been short of money but once it embraced Europe as its major cause it acquired its wealthiest patron to date, the European Commission Information Services (ECIS). Shrewdly CDS concentrated its efforts on the opinion-formers at every level in the Labour Party. These included office-holders in the constituency parties, trade union branch officials, and candidates in national or local elections. Its appeal was almost entirely to middle-class members of the party; it also had a good image with the younger members of the party. In effect CDS became a useful adjunct to the European Movement. The irony of the situation was that it had been founded to support an anti-Marketeer (Gaitskell) and had been dedicated to preserving the Anglo-American alliance.

It would be difficult to argue that CDS swung the Labour Party to apply for entry in 1967. It was hardly as simple as that. It was, however, an important factor which the European lobby both at home and abroad sensibly exploited. It is possible that Harold Wilson might have applied to join in 1967 without the existence of CDS in much the same way as Gaitskell would have applied in 1962, with possibly slightly more conviction on Wilson's part. But if George Brown and George Thomson had not been consistently supported by the CDS group they would have carried far less weight in the Labour Party. Some idea of the strength of CDS can be seen by a list of some of the young MPs in the 1966 and 1970 Parliaments who had at one time or another connections with the movement. They included Bill Rodgers, Dick Taverne, Roy Hattersley, Shirley Williams, Brian Walden, David Marquand, Ivor Richards, Allan Lee Williams, Jeremy Bray, John Smith, Donald Dowar, John Gilbert, Michael Barnes, Bob Maclennan, Philip Whitehead, Stanley Henig and

David Owens. From this group only Brian Walden and John Gilbert opposed the Conservative Party entry terms.

The Trade Unions

The CDS had connections with the trade union movement but these were neither numerous nor particularly effective. One of the undoubted strengths of the British trade union movement is its ability to ignore trendy middle-class thinking whether of the Left or the Right. Several of the trade unions were with CDS against unilateralism and a smaller number with CDS in favour of British entry into the EEC, but they have never been a majority of union membership.

The supporters of the Common Market within the trade union movement fall into two broad categories. There are the predominantly middle-class unions such as USDAW; and there are the professional anti-communists, of whom there are some representatives in most unions. The latter support the EEC largely because the Communist Party is opposed to it. An apparent exception to this broad categorization is the leadership of the GMW, the General and Municipal Workers. Most of the leaders of the GMW are keen pro-Marketeers: Fred Hayday was the GMW representative on the Labour Party NEC and thus probably the leading pro-Market trade unionist. However, the GMW leadership is quite unrepresentative of its membership on this issue.

Those trade unionists who support British membership of the EEC have had their resolve stiffened by their connections with the ICFTU (the international non-communist trade union organization) which provides frequent contacts with European trade unionists. Naturally enough nearly all trade unionists in the original Six were anxious for Britain to join the Market, both for its democratic traditions and its powerful union movement. There is a small question: who bore the cost of British trade unionists' visits to their continental colleagues? Certainly not the continental unions. Could it have been the Commission? Or the CIA?

The Wilson Era, 1964–70

Harold Wilson's memoirs cast very little light on what motivated him personally to apply for entry into the EEC in 1967. There is an open contradiction between the accounts of the Prime Minister and his Cabinet colleagues engaged in the negotiations.

It is obvious that those engaged in the negotiations are likely
to have had an almost professional interest that they should
succeed, so their commitment to British entry is not really so very
surprising. What seems to have been missing all along is any
irresistible pressure from either the Labour Party or the Parliamentary Labour Party to go in, so one must assume that there
were other factors which made Wilson decide in favour of entry
or at least making a show at negotiating entry terms (i.e. testing
the waters of Europe). Clearly a number of Wilson's Cabinet,
notably George Brown, Roy Jenkins and George Thomson,
would have accepted entry terms of any sort and trusted to
straighten things out from within. (The negotiations only touched
on the transitional period so the terms were virtually that Britain
entered the Community unconditionally.) But there was at no
point a majority of the Cabinet who would have forced through
entry against the wishes of the Prime Minister. Wilson's position
was not as strong as Heath's in 1971, but it was strong enough.

There are grounds for believing that Wilson, who was at no
stage an ardent European (not only because he valued the
Commonwealth as well as the European connection, but also
because he had been much closer to the feelings of the majority
of the British people on the issue), was much more seriously
influenced by the advice he received consistently from the Civil
Service (reinforced by the quality press) than any pressure from
within the party. By adopting a European stance, of course,
Wilson was robbing Heath of his most important foreign policy
card and also reducing the heat on his own administration from
the Opposition benches. Possibly, too, Wilson overestimated the
bargaining value of Britain's technological (especially aero-
nautical) and nuclear capacity at the conference table. He had
made a great play once before (1964) of the white heat of a
technological revolution, which might yet be able to be fulfilled
by pooling national resources in Europe. Finally, one cannot rule
out the extent to which he was taken in by what was an essentially Conservative argument, namely that Britain's entry would
restore her to a position at the top table. Certainly George Brown
seems to have been obsessed by this idea.

Nevertheless, whether Wilson was pushed from behind by
the Labour Party, or as seems more probable, enticed by the
beguiling voices of the civil servants in Whitehall (and Brussels),
the money spent by the Commission on the Labour Party was
well conceived and ultimately well spent. Had not General de

Gaulle vetoed the negotiations for a second time the pro-Marketeers in the Labour Party would have been well occupied in persuading Labour's grass roots that entry was right. As it turned out the minority section of the Labour Party was crucial to the Conservatives' majority in the Commons in 1971. Any person reading the press reports of the period will be struck by the consistency with which the Labour pro-Marketeers are reported and extensively quoted, out of all proportion to their supporters in the parliamentary party or the party at large. Speaking generally, the Community failed to win the complete trust of the Labour Party at any level. It did however win the support and unstinted co-operation of a significant body within the party, enough, as we have noted, to turn the parliamentary tide. Some idea of the extent to which Harold Wilson was assessing the possibility of staying outside the EEC is seen in Pickles' account of events which took place in 1964. Pickles relates: "By 1964 I was invited by Richard Marsh to meet Harold Wilson with a request to provide a more positive version of the anti-Market position. I declined, as being something I was not suited to compile. Later David Ennals [the International Committee Secretary] and Peter Shore set up a committee for a wider Europe with a campaign flowing from it. I suspect that Harold Wilson felt that if he could swing the Labour Party to withholding its fire against the US over Vietnam he could also swing Britain whatever way he wanted, whenever he wanted over the Common Market. At this particular period he was swinging markedly against."

The high point of his swing against was reached in his speech at Bristol which was strongly anti-Market (very possibly based on a draft by Peter Shore) and contained references to Mr Heath as a French poodle.

The question arises at what point and for what reasons did Harold Wilson swing to favouring entry. As Uwe Kitzinger rightly observes, Harold Wilson was one of the few people but for whom Britain could not have entered the Community. First, he committed the party to the principle of entry in 1967[1] thus keeping enlargement a live issue in the 60s and making entry much easier in the 70s. Second, had the Labour Party been opposed "on principle" in 1970 and had it not made the disengagements with the Commonwealth it is doubtful if the Conservative application would have succeeded.

As we have already noted, the Labour Party in general was

[1] *Diplomacy and Persuasion*, Thames and Hudson, 1973.

not too settled about the wisdom of entry to the Common Market in the very early part of the 1960s. Thus when Harold Wilson made a comprehensively negative speech in June 1962 it was significant both for what it said and for what it indicated about Left-wing attitudes within the party. His main attack was that the EEC was anti-planning in its ethos and therefore incompatible with British socialist thinking. Furthermore, the political prospects were not encouraging. In particular he feared the domination of Western Europe by a Paris-Bonn axis, intransigent towards the Soviet Union and eventually armed with nuclear weapons. It was in short the fear of a militarist and expansionist Germany bent on reunification that might drag Western Europe and its EEC partners in particular into yet another European war that held the darkest forebodings for him. Yet within four years he made a formal application for entry. The reasons for this apparent change of heart must of necessity be somewhat speculative but the influences which were brought to bear can at least be analysed.

As in 1962, prior to his June speech, Harold Wilson had been influenced by having dinner with some High Tories at the Dorchester, so when he came into office in 1964 he came under the influence of a now deeply committed Foreign Office (see the chapter on the Civil Service). Thus by 1964 he had already begun to move in his position to the point where he was looking for a more positive way of saying no. To this end he encouraged both Peter Shore, an avowed anti-Marketeer, and David Ennals, the former International Secretary of the Labour Party, to establish the Wider Europe Group.

On 10 November 1966, Harold Wilson, now Prime Minister with a substantial majority, called for a "great debate" on Britain and the prospects for her entering the Common Market. At the same time he announced his intention to visit the capitals of Western Europe, together with the then Foreign Secretary, George Brown, with the purpose of seeking membership if it were found to be consistent with the essential interests of Britain and the Commonwealth. The underlying premise of such a reconnaissance must have been to assess what changes had taken place since the previous application had been vetoed by General de Gaulle in 1963.

We have seen in the preceding chapter how much the Conservative leader was influenced by his top professional advisers, a theme amplified in the chapter on the Civil Service. The question is to what extent did the advice Harold Wilson was receiving from his top civil servants influence him in his conversion to EEC entry in 1966 and his gradual shift to rejecting the Tory terms of 1971 in favour of a renegotiation. While George Wigg's autobiography[2] mentions that Harold Wilson told him that he was persuaded in favour of entry by an article in *The Economist* on 22 October 1966, Lord Wigg believes that Wilson believed that it was the only means of holding the Cabinet together in the wake of the July financial crisis. By adopting a positive, businesslike stance towards British entry the Prime Minister was able to rally the support of the pro-Marketeers in the Cabinet, especially George Brown, and mollify the anti-Marketeers with the prospect that entering into negotiations, by revealing the precise terms of entry, would dispose of the issue once and for all. Since Wilson has always seen the role of Labour leader as one of holding a very diverse coalition together, the idea that a major factor in the first Labour Government application was to maintain that coalition in working order has about it a certain credibility that more specific incidental factors lack. As someone who had contested the leadership and who had threatened to resign in July 1966 George Brown had to be given a senior portfolio, and since he had always wanted it since 1964 the Foreign Office seemed an inevitable solution. Equally inevitably the appointment of Brown meant a fullhearted attempt to bring about British entry into the EEC. Though relations might be stormy, he was to prove a welcome reinforcement to the pro-Europeanist views already held by almost all the top officials at the Foreign Office. Indeed when Patrick Gordon-Walker first arrived at his Foreign Office desk he found a strongly pro-Market memo which purported to be an impartial briefing on the subject of Britain's policy towards Europe. To begin with he resisted this imposition of a view that was not his own but gradually he found himself fighting a losing battle as the need to lean on his department's resources left him making only minor modifications to the speeches that had been prepared for him.

As to the advice that Harold Wilson was personally exposed to, it was almost exclusively pro-Europeanist with the possible exception of Terry Pitt, head of the Labour Party Research Department, whose access to a Labour leader in office could hardly be described as close. A key influence on Wilson was

[2] Lord Wigg, *George Wigg*, Michael Joseph, London, 1972.

undoubtedly Sir Michael Palliser. Personally selected by the Prime Minister as Wilson's translator on his European "exploration" with George Brown, Palliser tended to confirm Wilson's interest in the immediate political advantages of entry and put on one side the economic consequences, whatever they might be. Moreover, since Palliser was a professional optimist, as was the Prime Minister, Palliser's influence grew. The suspicion remains that one of the consequences of Wilson's European tour was to increase his admiration for the sheer political acumen and nerve of President de Gaulle and to implant the thought that the General was not young and that if *he* could dominate the Community then perhaps when he had gone Wilson could, in his own very different style, manipulate its still weak institutions in the British interest. It is also possible that quite unconsciously Wilson wished to adopt a different course from that of Hugh Gaitskell in whose shadow he had grown to political maturity.

Perhaps the most powerful argument explaining the decision of Harold Wilson to apply for entry is that, like the Conservative Party in the wake of Suez, whose self-confidence had been shattered and who therefore sought an entirely new role, so the July 1966 financial crisis (only four months after he had gained a comfortable majority from the electorate) shook the Government's belief in Britain's economic survival outside the EEC. It was very much the national panacea psychology, even if the arguments that it was in fact a national panacea were to be deployed by the Conservative pro-Europeans rather than the Labour ones. Part of this pattern of withdrawal from Britain's formerly worldwide commitments was the decision to withdraw the British military presence East of Suez—actually taken at a Chequers weekend on Europe. Wilson's inability to solve the Rhodesian issue and the "stick" he received from some of the African Commonwealth states tended to underline the shrinking nature of British national power and prestige in the 1965-early 1966 period.

The tide was running in favour of the pro-Europeanists in the Cabinet in the autumn of 1966; thus it was no great surprise that on Saturday, 22 October at a Chequers meeting held to discuss European policy, George Brown and Michael Stewart, both avid supporters, presented a joint paper advocating entry. As with all such internal policy documents within all three major parties it was an almost exclusively political argument. Ever since the very early 1960s when cost-benefit analysis of British entry on economic grounds demonstrated a highly dubious case for entry (see the chapter on the Civil Service), the economic arguments deployed for public consumption had taken the form of either the vaguest kind of overall claims of economic benefits, usually from a "vast home market", or more detailed claims of benefits for particular interest groups or sections of the national economy. The latter were the more convincing arguments to professional economists or businessmen, though gradually the broader claims assumed wider and wider acceptance by sheer dint of persistence. At the Chequers meeting the Cabinet was still deeply divided, with Douglas Jay, Fred Peart, Barbara Castle, Richard Marsh, Richard Crossman and Anthony Wedgwood Benn either opposed outright or deeply sceptical about the wisdom of applying for entry. Those Ministers who advocated entry were not able to muster any very convincing economic arguments any more than had the civil servants who briefed the ministerial party in the morning. All in all there was no fresh evidence for submitting an application, nor was there overwhelming pressure within the Cabinet to do so.

Nevertheless it was at this weekend meeting that Harold Wilson proposed his tour of six capitals to be made by himself and George Brown to assess whether an entry bid could be made with any hope of obtaining satisfactory terms. On the face of it, it seemed a reasonable enough proposal. In fact such soundings could be undertaken by normal diplomatic channels. By undertaking such a high-level series of visits Wilson was to provide a degree of apparent commitment which was skilfully seized upon by the continental governments and the pro-Europeanists in Britain. By this act, which was announced to the House of Commons on 10 November, Harold Wilson ensured that he was to go down in history as the first Prime Minister to make formal application for entry (in 1967); he went on to describe his progress for entry "at one hell of a pace". Excepting Edward Heath, no other British political leader was to contribute so much to Britain's eventual entry. By January 1967 in a speech to the Council of Europe at Strasbourg Wilson spoke of Britain meaning business in seeking to help forge the unity of Europe; the tide of optimism was beginning to rise within him. Before the end of March the reconnaissance of the EEC capitals had been completed. During April the Cabinet considered a vast number of economic assessments, though given the degree of commitment that we shall examine in the chapter on the Civil Service, it is doubtful if these economic assessments were quite as searching as they may have appeared. Certainly Douglas Jay was far from satisfied with either their evidence or their conclusions. In the very last weekend in April the Cabinet met at Chequers to discuss informally two basic issues : first the strategic alternatives—whether it was in the British interest to join the EEC; to collaborate with the United States, Canada and EFTA in a free trade area which would invite the Six to join them later; or to "go it alone", known as GITA. Second, the tactical alternatives of whether to apply more or less unconditionally as Wilson and Brown proposed; whether to make a closely conditioned application; whether to postpone Britain's application until a more favourable moment; or to scrap any application altogether. In the event all these points of view had to be taken account of as representing views held within the Cabinet. On the central issue of whether Britain should or should not join, the Cabinet was equally divided. Those in favour included Harold Wilson, George Brown, Michael Stewart, Roy Jenkins, Anthony Crosland, Anthony Wedgwood Benn, Ray Gunter and Gerald Gardiner; those against, Douglas Jay, Fred Peart, Denis Healey, Barbara Castle, Richard Marsh, William Ross and Herbert Bowden. What was decisive in making an application was that for purely tactical reasons Jim Callaghan, Patrick Gordon-Walker and Richard Crossman were in favour of the Wilson-Brown application, primarily to dispose of the issue. The Chief Whip, John Silkin, also belonged to the sub-group of those tactically in favour of an application. Thus on 2 May 1967, the Wilson Cabinet took the formal decision to make an application for entry, a decision that was announced to the House of Commons later the same day. That this was carried out without a single resignation when the Cabinet was in fact equally divided over the final wisdom of joining is a tribute to the Prime Minister's managerial gifts. No doubt stemming from his tour of European capitals where everyone had stressed the traditional high purpose of the EEC, the goal of European unity, Wilson emphasized that his aim was to play a full part in the moves towards political unity. This marked a radical step forward in the British approach which hitherto, even under Macmillan, had always argued the case for entry (at least publicly) on grounds of greater freedom of trade. Ever since the EEC came into being critics of the goal of political unity have always asked, What form of political unity? The answer to that question is still not known and indeed is not remotely likely to be known until it happens, or fails to happen. Meanwhile the idea of exercising influence in world affairs as a result of this newly created political unity was a constant Wilsonian theme. The scarcely concealed hope of the Wilson application was that Britain would acquire a new world political influence by playing a major role in the European integration movement. The fact is that unlike in the Commonwealth, where Britain was at the very least *primus inter pares*, in the EC she would be the newest and, by the time she joined, among its weakest members.

It is of the utmost importance to record the bare fact that the Labour Cabinet, notwithstanding George Brown's emphatic claims that a Labour Cabinet would have entered the EEC but for the De Gaulle veto, never directly debated the issue of joining the EEC, only that of whether or not to apply to join. The stance was substantially the same as the Conservative promise "to negotiate; no more, no less", both Prime Ministers counting on a successful negotiation to transform an initial commitment merely to negotiate into one of commitment to the EEC. In the case of the Labour Prime Minister the moment of truth came with ultimate finality with the De Gaulle veto in December, and with it the collapse of the Government's chief foreign policy initiative.

Apart from the Soames Affair, which has been fully discussed elsewhere and underlined the continuing scepticism of De Gaulle towards the supranational institution of the Community, the issue became dormant until the publication of a Government White Paper in early 1970. It was a strange document which satisfied almost nobody. On the one hand the Foreign Office were unhappy because of the absence of any substantial political arguments for joining, on the other, although it purported to be an economic document (it was produced in the Cabinet Office), it deployed many unsupported statements and ended up by calculating the balance-of-payments burden at between £100m and £1,000m. Such a non-conclusion, while it enabled the Cabinet to approve it, hardly reflected the likelihood of the known adverse consequences on the balance of payments which, at least in the short term, nobody attempted to refute. The Labour Government then promised to enter into negotiations with the Six once more. Totally unexpectedly as far as the Prime Minister was concerned, the Labour Government were to be defeated in the election which took place twelve days before the negotiations opened. As if to emphasize the overriding role played by the Government machine, the Conservative Ministers, who had held office eight days only when the negotiations began, far from requesting a postponement (which the Six widely expected) merely picked up the Civil Service briefs prepared for their predecessors.

A further interesting feature of this period which Uwe Kitzinger's excellent book[3] on how Britain joined the Common Market examines with some skill is the tactics that Wilson was apparently going to use to enhance the prospects of a Labour Cabinet approving the terms. The negotiation briefs were never approved by a Labour Cabinet but would have manifestly needed to be approved before the negotiations commenced. Thus the negotiating terms would have had to be approved within the first week of Labour's presumed resumption of office, and when a Cabinet split was unthinkable. In pursuit of this timetable of events Harold Wilson instructed his Minister for Europe, George Thomson, and his private secretary, Crispin Tickell (later Anthony Barber's and then Geoffrey Rippon's private secretary) to finish the draft of his opening speech for swift approval by the Cabinet immediately following the election. Dictated in a Dundee hotel, this speech and its chief articles became the basis of Anthony Barber's Luxembourg speech for the Conservatives. The overall game plan reveals the tactical skills of Harold Wilson and the essentially bipartisan commitment that the Civil Service were able to impart to the leadership of both major parties whatever their public difference of emphasis might be.

Against all predictions, or almost all, the Labour Party went down to defeat on 19 June 1970. Among the most notable electoral casualties on the Labour side was the deputy leader and leading pro-Marketeer, George Brown. He was however succeeded as deputy leader by an equally ardent advocate of entry in Roy Jenkins, while in the Shadow Cabinet as a whole the pro-Marketeers were more than adequately represented. At a less elevated level, the grass roots of the Labour Party in the shape of the party activists in general and the trade unions in particular, took the election defeat as their cue to express what had always been their predominant feeling about the EEC, that of overriding scepticism. By September 1970, when the Labour Party conference met, followed by the Trades Union Congress,

3 Uwe Kitzinger, *Diplomacy and Persuasion*, Thames & Hudson, 1973.

the tide was beginning to flow strongly against entry among the ranks of the Labour Party. There had in fact never been a true majority in favour of actual entry.

Peter Shore, already a redoubtable anti-Marketeer and almost unique in that he was to be the only Cabinet Minister from either major party who did not effectively come under the sway of his Civil Service advisers once the negotiations were under way, came out on the eve of the Labour conference in total opposition. He put his finger on the new barriers to British entry which had not previously existed, namely that the Common Agricultural Policy had now come fully into effect and the plans for an economic and monetary union were more far-reaching than anything Britain had remotely contemplated previously.

Adding a groundswell to Shore's warnings and making the party leadership think seriously again was the evidence that only about 20 per cent of the electorate were in favour of entry while no party so far represented the remaining 80 per cent who were either doubtful or opposed. Anthony Wedgwood Benn appeared to be riding two horses in late 1970, the one headed for entry into the Community, the other urging a referendum which at that time would have undoubtedly overwhelmingly rejected entry. It was a more honest position than many people gave him credit for since it said that as a technocratic minister he could see advantages to entry for Britain, but that on the other hand it was too fundamental a decision to go ahead with against the popular will. His call for a referendum, part of his general belief in greater participation in both industry and government, while it could not be implemented until the third Wilson Government was formed, was also, although not an ideal method, the last chance to convey a degree of legitimacy to whatever decision was taken. As we see quite clearly in this book, at no general election prior to British entry was this issue, of unparalleled magnitude in peacetime, ever squarely put to the electorate. When the tides of inflation and unemployment threaten the life of established order and institutions, there is a clear onus for any government to demonstrate the legitimacy of any major undertaking to which the mere evoking of Edmund Burke's views on the role of a member of parliament is at best irrelevant and at worst an offence. It should also be noted that Douglas Jay, who also favoured a referendum, had, like Benn, maintained an overall consistency of approach to the principle of participation in other matters : witness his chairmanship of London's Anti-Motorway

Box which was another "people versus the bureaucrats and vested interests" confrontation. The idea that the issue was too complex to be submitted to the people's verdict was in fact a more or less unchallenged assumption shared by the advocates of entry in all three parties and above all by the Civil Service. Remarkable as it may seem, up until the beginning of 1971 the most forceful advocates of entry had managed to avoid admitting what they held as a commonplace privately, namely that they wished to gain British entry under any terms, in the belief that the Community could be remoulded from within. During the course of 1971 this stark truth began to seep through to the parliamentary ranks of the Labour Party. Beginning in January the Tribune group managed to raise 132 signatures of an Early Day motion: "That this House believes that entry into the EEC on the terms so far envisaged would be against the interests of this country", while in February Wilson warned the Six that Britain could afford to stay out if the terms were too tough. Nevertheless, right up until May there had been no movement by the Six on offering more generous transitional arrangements for New Zealand and the Caribbean, as well as Britain, which is all the negotiations were in fact concerned with. By May too it was estimated that no more than forty or so Labour MPs were regarded as firmly in favour of entry. The situation was fast arising when the vast majority of Labour MPs were firmly against with a substantial proportion of the Shadow Cabinet, including the Leader of the Opposition, left high and dry in favour not only of entry but of what had become the keystone of the Heath Government. Something had to give and it was the party leader, who had always seen the preservation of the party as his top priority, who was bound to shift his ground. His position became more concentrated on the terms and he began to reiterate that if the terms were prohibitive no British Government could join. It was apparent already that the Labour leader would not find the Tory terms acceptable.

Responding to these undercurrents from the rank and file members of the Parliamentary Labour Party, the Labour Committee for Europe splashed a full-page advertisement in the *Guardian* extolling the virtues of British entry in the widest possible terms as promoting "the causes of social democracy, world peace and economic advance in both developed and developing countries". Such sweeping claims, embracing un-exceptionable goals, were so far above any means of testing their validity that their significance obviously lay in their signatories. They comprised 200 Labour MPs (including eight members of the Shadow Cabinet)—it was not difficult to sign such an anodyne statement—and a clutch of leading continental social democrats including Willy Brandt, Guy Mollet and Pietro Nenni. The statement illustrated what we saw much earlier in this chapter, namely that when European socialists got together they had to confine things to generalities unless their practical political differences were to become exposed. By the end of May, Jim Callaghan, with a profound consciousness of the swing against the Common Market within the Labour Party and possibly aware that he might capture the initiative from Wilson, made a speech at Southampton which was very critical about the dangers of bad entry terms. With the prospect of a parliamentary veto in October the anti-Marketeers pressed for a special conference on 17 July to settle an issue which was obviously divisive and which the anti-Marketeers knew, if taken to a vote, would demonstrate a clear majority against. The Labour Party Executive narrowly approved the demand for such a conference. The month of July 1971 marked the turn of the tide as far as the anti-Marketeers in the party were concerned; nevertheless the pro-Marketeers conducted a skilful rearguard action salvaging considerable face largely thanks to the skilful efforts of Harold Wilson in avoiding a head-on confrontation between the two rival Market factions. A BBC2 and BBC1 half-hour debate held on 13 July, while it may have confirmed many on both sides in their previous points of view, won round the studio audience to an anti-Market position. Then on 17 July the special party conference was held at Westminster Hall; the same morning a press conference in a House of Commons committee room launched a symposium, *Destiny or Delusion* (edited by Douglas Evans, published by Gollancz) representing a collection of essays by academics and politicians from both parties. Among the most notable essays was one by Nicholas Kaldor, Professor of Economics at Cambridge University and former economic adviser to the first Wilson Government. His essay on "The Dynamic Effects of the Common Market" had earlier caused a considerable stir when it was first published in the *New Statesman* under Richard Crossman's editorship. Reinforced by eleven other specialist contributors *Destiny or Delusion* was sent to around half of all MPs and helped to provide a solid expression of the fear that it was not only the short-term economic consequences of entry but also the long-term, both economic and political, which held out doubtful prospects of benefits for Britain. In the cry by many pro-Marketeers for cost-benefit analysis of the effects of entry it is remarkable that with all their financial resources at their disposal it was left to two anti-Marketeers in Kaldor and Peter Oppenheimer of Christchurch, Oxford, in an essay on "The Problem of Monetary Union",[4] to marshal the most convincing analysis of the dangers for Britain. Certainly both their efforts were more academically sound pieces of evidence than any of the White Papers produced by the Civil Service for their government on the economic consequences. As for the political arguments, they were kept at the level of vague assertions on the part of the pro-Marketeers for the simple reason that nobody knew in which direction the Community would evolve.

Meanwhile the special party conference was fraught with great dangers for the leadership, not least that the leadership would be overwhelmed from the floor in a tidal wave of outright opposition to the Market. With his usual backroom skills, Harold Wilson sounded out the unions (whose delegates wielded the majority of disposable votes) before the conference began to ensure that the debate did not bind the parliamentary leadership and remained a consultative exercise. Thus when Alfred Morris proposed a vote on a resolution openly opposing entry and calling for a General Election, a veto which if held would have been overwhelmingly carried, as the pro-Marketeers privately readily admitted, it was defeated by a 10 per cent majority. Thus came about the debate which followed in which pro- and anti-Market speakers alternately gave both sides an equal say, grossly overstating to the television viewer the numerical support of the pro-Marketeers in the party as reflected in an overwhelming vote against in the TUC Congress. If George Thomson was to claim that the Tory terms would have been approved by a Labour Cabinet, which will forever remain an arguable proposition, Peter Shore made the counter-claim that the terms were "appallingly" bad, adding that claims that entry would increase the prosperity of Britain were "flagrantly dishonest". Wilson's closing speech conveyed the clear impression that he for one thought the terms were unacceptable. Ten days later the National Executive Committee passed a tough resolution opposing the Tory terms (by 16 to 6) and decided to support

[4] Douglas Evans (ed.), *Britain in the EEC* (Gollancz, 1973).

their resolution with a national campaign. Though the party conference was not to lend its support until October, the collective leadership of the Labour Party had already made up its mind to resist accepting the terms negotiated. Yet within the Shadow Cabinet there was an open group of dissenters led by Roy Jenkins and including Shirley Williams, Harold Lever and George Thomson.

Beginning in the spring of 1971 this group of pro-Marketeers within the Shadow Cabinet were given an almost ceaseless coverage by Fleet Street, out of all proportion to their support in the parliamentary party. Both at the Reform Club where they met for working lunches in a private dining room and in Jenkins' room in the House (just opposite Harold Wilson's) "Sir Roy and his Knights of the Round Table" as they became known, assumed a distinctly Bloomsbury Group image. Meanwhile Douglas Houghton, the party chairman but also a pro-Marketeer, was able to liaise with the Conservatives, especially on such matters as the necessity of having a free vote. This was to prove a crucial tactical play in the October vote and one which Jenkins' "lieutenant" William Rodgers played a major role in promoting. Even more important was Rodgers collecting a group of around sixty-nine Labour MPs who would vote with the Government on 26 October, a group who, together with the twenty Labour MPs who abstained, gave the Tories a majority.

By comparison with the special conference in July the continuation of the internecine struggle at the Party Conference at Brighton was of secondary importance. After two pre-conference rallies organized respectively by the Labour Committee for Safeguards on the Common Market and the Labour Committee for Europe, the EEC debate was held on the first day of the conference proper. The general reasoning was that this scheduling was likely to minimize any threat to the Executive's plan, which was now chiefly bent on salvaging party unity. The debate ended with a speech from Jim Callaghan who pointed out that Mr Heath had apparently accepted both the Common Agricultural Policy and the plans for an Economic and Monetary Union and that the Labour Party accepted neither. On the very night that the Executive motion was passed by a 5:1 majority (essentially a rejection of Tory terms), the pro-Marketeers leaked to the press the fact that they could muster very nearly seventy votes to add to those of the Government in voting for the terms on offer. When Harold Wilson spoke he not only urged party unity, but in a subtle recognition of the inevitability of defections on the day, spoke of the need to unite on the mass of consequential legislation during 1972.

On 18 October the Prime Minister played what in tactical terms was his trump card; he let it be known that at least on the Government benches, he would allow a free vote. As we have seen in the chapter on the Conservative Party it was more apparent than real, a great deal of constituency pressure and party patronage pressure having already been applied with sufficient success to guarantee an overall majority on the assumption of a sizable Labour bloc voting with the Government. In the debate which began in the House of Commons on 21 October, the Tories had, by the mere act of allowing a free vote, acquired a psychological initiative which was to help emphasize the divisions of the Labour Party. The Labour leadership was left with the consolation of what later became known as the "Houghton doctrine" (after the Parliamentary Party Chairman), the principle that whichever way a Labour member voted on the vote of principle he was honour-bound to support the Labour Party majority view (an overwhelming majority at that in both the parliamentary and national parties) in all the consequential legislation that was expected to flow from it in 1972. The vote of 28 October described earlier in this book, was already more or less decided in practical terms though the air of uncertainty persisted right up until the very last moment.

Although the Labour Party lost the contest in the vote on the principle of entry in the autumn of 1971, and lost considerable face with its supporters for "allowing" a major revolt to be effectively expressed, in the purely tactical sense of fulfilling the role of an opposition the Labour Party was well placed. It was overwhelmingly critical of the entry terms that the Conservative Party and a minority of its own party found acceptable. This meant the party leadership could press for a renegotiation of the terms as its policy both in opposition and in office, not merely as a tactic to hold the party together, though it certainly had that effect, but as an expression of grass roots dissatisfaction with not only the terms but the manner in which they were obtained. In the chapter on the Civil Service we shall see how the pro-Marketeers, but even more the Civil Service departments, operating in concert, exploited the twin basic needs of the Labour Government both to maintain unity and to produce a package which looked like an acceptable bargain to the British electorate.

Meanwhile the Labour leader, since March 1974 Prime Minister once again, found himself reassessing his attitudes to the EEC. After handing over the renegotiations to the Foreign Secretary, James Callaghan, Wilson began to see the Community in a more favourable light as time wore on. The appeal of the German Chancellor Herr Schmidt and his conception of the EEC as an intergovernmental agency cannot be underestimated. This was helped by the fact that the Labour Party tends in general to get on with Germany and with the Social Democrats in particular. Finally, remembering the traumas of the 1966 monetary crisis, Harold Wilson could hardly ignore the spectre of Sheik Yamani withdrawing the Arab sterling balances if Britain should opt for a withdrawal. It was a piece of pro-Market bluffmanship, since Sheik Yamani was free to do so for all sorts of reasons, but it was the kind of nightmare that would haunt any British Prime Minister for some time.

III

THE CIVIL SERVICE

THE REPUTATION OF the British Civil Service stands among the highest of any in the world. This justly-deserved reputation for justice, probity and general high standards has stood the test of time in the face of ham-fisted governments and a general suspicion of a growth in bureaucracy as governments everywhere assume more and more responsibility for the conduct of affairs. Nevertheless, a distinctive feature of the British governmental system is the persistent cloak of secrecy which it casts about its activities. Nowhere is this more true than in the conduct of foreign policy. There is undoubtedly considerable justification for conducting the day-to-day practice of diplomacy on a mutually confidential basis. However, when this confidentiality is extended to the process of formulating and executing major aspects of foreign policy in a peacetime era there must be some cause for concern. It is worth observing at the outset that institutions rather than people lie at the heart of this secretive tradition. Accordingly, if we are to understand the pattern of events and the decision-making process within the Civil Service, and more especially the Foreign Office, the Treasury, the Ministries of Agriculture and of Trade and the Cabinet Office, which culminated in Britain's entry into the EEC, then we need to sketch in briefly the institutional structure within which British foreign policy is devised. Within the framework of the European Liaison group, an interdepartmental official committee representing all five departments, the permanent officials played an indispensable role in Britain's foreign policy towards the EEC, not least in the provision of continuity, as well as acting as a think-tank on this single major issue.

There are perhaps half a dozen summary points that can usefully be made about the framework within which British foreign policy is devised. First, both in law and in practice the conduct of foreign policy is the undivided responsibility of the Executive, meaning the Cabinet and the civil service departments most concerned. Second, unlike the case of the US

President, who is specifically invoked to seek both the advice and consent of the Congress, there is only a general obligation on the Executive to carry Parliament, often, if the policy is devised in secret, long after it has been set in motion. There is, specifically, a notable lack of any even remote equivalent of the Senate Committee for Foreign Relations. Third, the only sense in which there is other than a fortuitous and occasional check on foreign policy by the legislative branch of government is in its financial aspects. Here the Select Committee on the Estimates subjects foreign policy to a very indirect and imprecise form of parliamentary review. Fourth, the House of Commons, while it stages set-piece debates on foreign policy and of course demands that the Foreign Secretary makes himself available from time to time to answer questions, exercises the very minimum of control over major policy direction if only because it is evolved almost entirely behind closed doors. With the Commons so minimally informed, the Executive is left in virtual monopoly control over not only the execution of foreign policy, which is its right, but also its primary formulation, which is not its exclusive right by any means, particularly as it impinges on domestic policy to an increasing extent. Fifth, while the Cabinet as a whole is technically the supreme executive organ for the formulation and conduct of foreign policy, in practice most foreign policy is discussed in the appropriate Cabinet committee, especially the all-powerful Defence and Overseas Policy Committee, normally chaired by the Prime Minister himself. Moreover, of great significance in a highly specialist yet wide-ranging field such as foreign affairs, both the Cabinet and the Defence and Overseas Policy Committee deliberate on the basis of information supplied by the departmental officials concerned. Thus every Minister in the overseas policy field is to a greater or lesser extent in the hands of his permanent officials. While in domestic ministries the Minister may often fall back on what his party outlined in their election manifesto as the guidelines for the policy he may wish to pursue, in foreign affairs manifestos tend to be long on general principles and high-sounding phrases and short on specific policy goals and commitments. This is almost inevitable given that a government of any middle-sized power has only a modest influence over its external environment, but it has the quite concrete effect of strengthening the hand of the permanent officials at the expense of the Minister. Sixth, it is above all the Prime Minister himself who in modern Britain has the controlling hand on foreign policy. He achieves this indirectly by the appointment of the Ministers most concerned with foreign policy—the Foreign Secretary, the Chancellor of the Exchequer, the Defence Secretary, the Minister of Trade, the Minister of Agriculture and the Minister of Overseas Development; and directly by his chairmanship of the Cabinet and more often than not the regular meetings of the Defence and Overseas Policy Committee. As if to emphasize this point Prime Minister Heath had his pre-entry Government White Paper on Europe prepared by the Cabinet Office (Permanent Secretary, Sir William Neild) as a presumed neutral referee to the competing departmental interests. Not that the dominance of British Prime Ministers in the conduct of foreign policy is in the nature of a secret. Not since Stanley Baldwin abdicated his foreign policy role to his Foreign Secretary in the 1930s has any British Prime Minister done anything but conduct his own foreign policy, at least in its basic directions. Meetings between heads of governments have become so much an integral element in contemporary international relations that it could hardly be otherwise. Even though Ernest Bevin, whom some regard as the most formidable Foreign Secretary since Lord Salisbury, exercised a considerable degree of autonomy under Attlee, not merely because of his undoubted skill as a statesman but because of his substantial political power-base in his own right, the evidence is overwhelming that he consulted Attlee on all major policy questions. In the postwar period Eden, Macmillan and Heath each exercised a very tight control over the conduct of foreign affairs. Eden in particular was all-powerful not least because his experience in foreign affairs in general and European affairs in particular exceeded that of his permanent officials. His downfall at Suez may in part be attributed to an over-reliance on his own personal expertise and an inability to stand the strain of the political and parliamentary holocaust that he unleashed upon himself. Although his failure to prosecute the Suez expedition to its military conclusion alienated France from Britain almost as much as the original enterprise had soured relations between France and the United States, which had effectively blocked the Anglo-French intervention), it underlined the inability of Britain to pursue a course of war independently of the United States rather than any inherent weakness in the office of Prime Minister, which had long since ceased to be that of *primus inter pares*. Thus to summarize the structure in which major aspects of British foreign policy are formulated and carried out, it can be said unequivocally that the Prime Minister is normally supremo. That being so whenever the Foreign Office, or more specifically its top officials and (quite as relevant for foreign policy) those of the Treasury, have a major policy to promulgate —and they would be less than human if they never did, whatever constitutional theory lays down—the crucial man they need to enlist is the Prime Minister. If he gives his wholehearted support to any foreign policy initiative then all else follows in its train. Though it is handy to have the support of the other members of the Defence and Overseas Policy Committee, who would normally include the Foreign Secretary, the Chancellor, the Defence Secretary and the Minister of Trade, it is the Prime Minister who alone really counts.

During the period that this chapter confines itself to (from 1957 to 1975, with special emphasis on 1960 to 1970), the Foreign Office succeeded brilliantly in carrying with them each successive Prime Minister from Macmillan to Heath on the question of British entry. In the case of Macmillan, although he was heavily predisposed he saw that there was a balance of credit and loss to weigh up so he still had to be convinced—which he was, most emphatically, largely on advice from within the ranks of the Permanent Secretaries. Douglas-Home was a convert from about the same period, if a less enthusiastic one in the early stages. Harold Wilson stands out as a definite long-time sceptic who assuredly was profoundly influenced by the FO argument, even if the precise moment of his conversion is unclear. Edward Heath needed no persuading to back the efforts of the FO.

In such a brief analysis of the structure within which British foreign policy is hammered out it is impossible to do justice to all the influences that are brought to bear, ranging from the various government departments to influential lobbies like Chatham House, the International Institute for Strategic Studies etc., not to mention the CBI, the TUC and foreign embassies. Overshadowing all other impressions which might help to explain the British foreign policy structure, its scope, its secrecy, its praetorian guard ethos, is the inescapable fact that it represents the vestiges of an imperial heritage. It is moreover not too fanciful to imagine that a finely-tuned diplomatic machine like the FO found itself looking for new fields to conquer as Britain's worldwide empire was gradually run down. Not unnaturally, when the newly-formed EEC began to prosper it was seen as the obvious outlet for the FO's creative energies : "an empire on our doorstep" was a private phrase that summed up the feelings of not a few FO officials at the time. As bureaucrats they understood the "new Europe" which was beginning to take shape far better than the majority of British parliamentarians. Fanciful or not, what is indisputable is that throughout the 1960s and the early 1970s, the FO turned its energies wholeheartedly towards the promotion of British entry into the EEC. It seemed to many FO men the only available means open to Britain to remain a great power in the world, something that their whole training and experience had taught them Britain was destined to remain. They were not, however, alone in their unwillingness to conceive that Britain might have a bright future as a middle-sized power, less influential politically but a good deal more sleek economically, and with a honed-down foreign service. The politicians no less than the bureaucrats were on the whole slow to realize the extent to which British political and economic strength had declined, not so much in absolute terms but in relation to the two superpowers, not to mention Japan, West Germany and France.

Throughout most of the postwar period Britain has witnessed a deterioration in both the terms of trade and the relative value of its currency. It has been the misfortune of the British Civil Service that during this same postwar period it has been given the impossible task of reconciling a set of broadly irreconcilable objectives in the shape of full employment, a fixed rate of exchange, a stable domestic currency and one of the most comprehensive social security systems in the world. Many of the social goals set by Beveridge which were to be achieved by Keynesian economic principles were both desirable and achievable, but gradually, under the pressure of rising expectations they were upped beyond any realistic possibility of fulfilment. To take the most basic example, though Beveridge was anxious to avoid any repetition of the extraordinarily harsh unemployment of the 1930s his aim of guaranteeing unemployment benefits to all did not anticipate that the British work force would come increasingly to expect employment to be brought to them and not vice versa. Against such an expectation and the complementary one that it was the Government's overriding responsibility to maintain the lowest possible rate of unemployment, the expansion of the money supply and the consequent growth of endemic inflation had about it an air of inevitability.

While all these factors were present to varying degrees throughout the postwar period, the impossibility of reconciling rapid growth with low unemployment and sound money without some form of conscious trade-off between the three was scarcely appreciated. What began to preoccupy the Whitehall mandarins, and especially those at the Treasury, was Britain's low growth rate compared with her Continental neighbours. It was clear that their comparatively better performance was due to a great variety of factors, among them a consistently higher rate of investment, far greater labour mobility (much of it from migrant labour imported from outside the EEC), and what was then considered the most crucial factor of all, a larger home market than was apparently available to Britain. While it is perfectly true that almost all the postwar success stories among the nations of the western world based their prosperity on export-led growth, the existence of a substantial home market was far from being uniformly the case. Nevertheless the belief in the indispensability of a very large home market grew and was assiduously cultivated by many of the top Whitehall economic advisers. The paramount position of the Treasury in relation to all other government departments tended to accelerate the adoption of the belief that if Britain could only acquire an expanded home market she would be well on the road to an industrial revival. From the Treasury, therefore, far from in unison but nevertheless persistently, there came siren voices counselling that if Britain would only join the emerging Continental group based on the Treaty of Rome her economic renaissance would be guaranteed. This was most certainly the advice that Macmillan received from at least one of his joint Permanent Secretaries at the Treasury.

It is always an exercise fraught with danger to interpret broad and complex historical trends too heavily in terms of the people who happen to occupy the great political offices at the time these events come to a form of conclusion. If this is true of those in elected office it is even more so with those permanent officials whose expertise is often immensely greater than that of the Ministers they serve. Nevertheless, we cannot simply ignore their existence as if they were mere cyphers of their Minister's wills since they manifestly, and quite reasonably, were nothing of the kind. On the contrary, they compare favourably with most other bureaucratic élites with the sole exception of the top French technocrats who have earnt for themselves a legendary reputation for administrative skill and who operate in an environment wholly different from their British cousins.

Among those top officials who most affected British foreign policy in the years 1960 to 1975 there were around seven who stand out as exercising a crucial influence on Britain's decision to enter and on the tactics employed to make that decision a reality. Curiously enough only one of these, Sir Denis Greenhill (now Lord Greenhill), was ever Permanent Head of the Foreign Office. Of the others—Sir Frank Lee (Permanent Secretary at the Treasury), Sir Eric Roll (Permanent Secretary at the Department of Economic Affairs), Sir Con O'Neill (Deputy Permanent Secretary at the Foreign Office) and Sir William Armstrong (Permanent Secretary at the Treasury, later Head of the Civil Service, now Lord Armstrong)—all except O'Neill held economic ministries. Only Sir Christopher Soames in Paris and Lord Harlech in Washington served as what one might call "political" diplomats—though Sir Con served as Britain's chief professional negotiator in Brussels, having previously worked there as UK Ambassador to the EEC.

The question arises: why did these predominantly economic officials play so large and influential a role in the formulation of foreign policy? The answer is fundamentally twofold. First, because of the dominance of the Treasury over all other departments in the British Civil Service. Second, because if the decision to enter was made by each of Macmillan, Wilson and Heath on the broadest of political grounds, it needed both psychologically and practically to be supported by the best economic advice available within the Civil Service.

First, the pre-eminence of the Treasury over all other departments, including the Foreign Office: this fundamental feature of the British Civil Service arises from the fact that the British Treasury is not only responsible for long-range economic planning and the drawing-up of the Budget but also the general supervision of the expenditure of all other government departments. To give some idea of the sheer overwhelming concentration of power that this represents, a brief comparison with the US Department of the Treasury is helpful. First, the President as Chief Executive appoints (and dismisses) the Secretary of the Treasury who is wholly accountable to him. Second, the President is advised on overall economic strategy by the Council of Economic Advisers. Third, there is a Bureau of the Budget which exists quite independently of the Treasury. Fourth, the US

Treasury has no direct supervisory role over other major US Government Departments. For all these reasons the US Treasury is, by comparison with the British Treasury, far from being in any position to dictate policy to other major departments except under quite exceptional circumstances.

Second, while the merely budgetary aspects of the Foreign Office expenditure are fairly insignificant (around one-tenth of the Defence budget is about normal), the economic effects of a successful or unsuccessful foreign policy are likely to be crucial to the health of the economy of a nation as dependent on trade as Britain has traditionally been regarded. It is not without some significance that, in Treasury terms, the budgets for Defence and External Relations are considered together, as one might expect from their being overseen within the Cabinet by the Defence and Overseas Policy Committee. Not unnaturally there was a tendency within this Committee to equate, rather loosely, closer economic links with the countries of Western Europe with benefits to Britain's national security; it was then but a short step to associate closer institutional economic links with increased prosperity. It was within just this framework of considering Britain's defence and external relations together that the Treasury found itself having to make up its mind on the benefits and disadvantages of Britain joining the newly emerging EEC. It was not therefore surprising that the Treasury might eventually have to make up its mind on the issue far more on political than economic grounds. Equally predictably, it was also true that since it *was* the Treasury, it would have to promote whatever side of the political fence it came down on in the form of a particular economic set of arguments. To begin with, that is from 1957 to 1960, it was not at all sure which side it favoured, the supranationalists who wanted Britain to join the EEC or the political minimalists *cum* free traders who merely wanted a framework for increased trade and more regular political consultation between the existing national state structures. In the late 1950s the Treasury still had an open mind on the subject. Although by the mid-1960s the Treasury had, by and large, come down on the side of the supranationalists they thought of themselves as economic expansionists—which was more appealing than the thought of supplanting Britain's national political institutions which, unlike those of most of the continental powers, had survived the war intact. This emphasis on economic expansion rather than the eventual transfer of power to an international bureaucracy was vital to the entire operation of selling the Common Market to the British people and its various interest groups. But first there had to be a genuine debate on the subject —within the Civil Service. No less an authority than Lord Armstrong, former head of the Civil Service has asserted many times that the Civil Service is a great debating society, a fact borne out by the top brass of the Treasury at this time. It is assumed, however, when great issues of undoubted complexity arise, that if they are debated within the Civil Service then this will be enough. Indeed, the Civil Service goes much further and maintains that this is all that is possible in practical terms. At least this is, in very broad terms, the prevalent attitude among the top echelons of the Service.

In constitutional theory Permanent Under Secretaries are there to execute the political directives of their departmental Ministers and to provide them with the best possible professional advice. In practice it is widely accepted that they have a major and often decisive say in the formulation of policy. Since Ministers are usually in charge of departments for on average about three years, often only two, while civil servants often spend their entire professional careers in the same department, this is hardly surprising. It probably takes an able Minister a minimum of six months to master his role, a less able one twelve months—assuming he ever does—during which period the Permanent Under Secretary and his staff are bound to assert a formulative role in the creation of policy. Later, when the Minister has mastered the ropes, habits in decision-making have been formed on both sides which are often hard to break. Where an issue straddles more than one department, as the issue of Britain's entry into the EEC clearly did, this becomes accentuated as two or more Permanent Secretaries put their heads together and pool their strength. This is more readily achieved informally, but even the system of official committees of top civil servants which exactly parallel the major Cabinet Committees tends to boil issues down to their essentials and provide the corresponding Cabinet Committee with essentially predigested briefs and conclusions. If they are to avoid a surfeit of wear and tear and what they often regard as "purely political debate"— the phrase comes from the lips of innumerable officials—it is in the interests of most departmental officials to reach agreement at the level of the Cabinet Committee which then requires merely formal approval by the Cabinet. By such means only those issues which genuinely divide the civil servants themselves, or alternatively are manifestly politically contentious and too hot to handle, are passed on to the Cabinet. But if a department holds a united view, it is very much easier to exert influence on the policy making process. This tendency is reinforced by the fact that busy departmental Ministers have too little time to take up matters lying outside their departmental jurisdiction. This applies most emphatically of all in the field of foreign policy. As Dr Bruce Headley points out in his book on *British Cabinet Ministers* (Allen & Unwin, 1975), the majority of Ministers see the Cabinet more as an inter-departmental battleground than as a form for collective deliberation on policy. A majority of ex-Ministers interviewed also apparently expressed the view that many policy issues had been foreclosed within the inter-departmental official Whitehall committees long before they reached the Cabinet.

It is on these very same official committees that the Treasury can exert a disproportionate influence with its overall knowledge and control of total government expenditure. Thus within the Civil Service the permanent officials at the top are able to exert a twofold pressure : first, by offering their departmental Minister advice they have evolved steadily over a very long time and which is in consequence that much harder for him to resist; and second, by preparing official papers within the prestigous inter-departmental official committees, which, as the late Richard Crossman points out in his memoirs, are practically irresistible unless opposed by the Prime Minister or possibly the Chancellor. Of course when the Prime Minister and the top officials of the Civil Service share the same major objectives and the same assumption as to the means to be employed to achieve these goals they cannot be brooked. Some departments, most notably the Treasury, the Foreign Office and the Home Office have continuing long-range issues towards which they are bound in practical terms to develop basic attitudes regardless of what government is in power. The Common Market is such an issue *par excellence*, and the Treasury and Foreign Office were the two departments most involved from the very beginning.

All of the preceding description of the institutional structures of Whitehall, the committee system and the general procedures from which policy papers emerge is intended to clarify the general assertion that in practice a great deal of policy derives from the permanent officials rather than, as in constitutional theory, being handed down from the elected Minister. This feature of the British governmental process is far from being unique. Indeed, it is an inescapable fact that a very high proportion of the decisions that shape the EEC day by day are made by relatively low-ranking officials of the EEC Commission in Brussels. This is the more readily accomplished by the fact that the powers of scrutinization exercised by the European Parliament are quite inadequate to cope with the torrent of regulations that the Commission devises. In Britain, the bureaucracy is technically much more accountable to Parliament, though in practice, as we have seen, the powers of scrutinization of the legislative branch need a considerable overhaul (Question Time being loaded in favour of the Executive with its departmental back-up), to say nothing of the deficiencies of the Cabinet system as currently practised. Nevertheless, it would be quite wrong to suggest that these deficiencies are all on the side of the civil servants, or even of the Civil Service structure. A great deal that could be improved lies on the political side of the fence. It goes without saying that some very able parliamentary performers are far from capable administrators of great departments of state. Moreover others, though personally able, cannot absorb enough, quickly enough, on subjects that they are not sufficiently steeped in beforehand. Nowhere is a lack of prior knowledge in depth more likely to make the Minister more dependent on his departmental advisers than in foreign affairs—unless in the Treasury, where confidentiality is deemed essential in economic forecasting, as with the facts upon which it is based.

All of this may help to explain the significance of the arrival in January 1960 of the first of the seven officials named earlier, Sir Frank Lee, as joint Permanent Under Secretary at the Treasury. A strong personality with a correspondingly forceful manner, Sir Frank was an Australian who believed firmly, even at this early stage, that British industry could never succeed without the sort of expanded home market which the EEC apparently seemed to provide (this being before the Kennedy Round had successfully lowered industrial tariff barriers during the mid-1960s). With missionary zeal Sir Frank went about the conversion of the top people in both government and private industry. His success was spectacular. Before long he had gained the endorsement of the Federation (later Confederation) of British Industries and it soon became fashionable to talk of Britain's need to improve her growth rate. The Economic Steering Committee (one of the key official inter-departmental committees which, as we have already seen, frequently pre-empt decisions before they even reach the Cabinet by presenting a united Whitehall approach) was then chaired by Sir Frank; after weighing up the pros and cons, it concluded that Britain ought to seek entry into the EEC. Significantly, however, the grounds advanced were mostly political rather than economic, though there was a widespread expectation that the prospect of political advance would somehow give a psychological fillip to the morale of British industrialists. The truth is that, in strictly statistical terms, as early as 1960 it was clear that there could be no guaranteed or even clear economic benefits accruing to Britain as a nation from entry. Why the Economic Steering Committee decided that entry was desirable on political grounds and on what precise political grounds they decided is a major unanswered question. Perhaps the Economic Steering Committee knew that Macmillan would grasp at the chance of a major political initiative which would create a new field of endeavour and greatly please the Americans (as we shall see in the final chapter, though John Fitzgerald Kennedy had not yet been inaugurated, the US State Department was already beginning to promote British entry strongly). Certainly, whatever the political reasons advanced, by the end of 1960, the most coveted convert of all, Prime Minister Harold Macmillan, was convinced by Sir Frank's arguments and began to set to work to convince his Cabinet and ultimately the Conservative Party.

The conversion of the Foreign Office was even more easily accomplished. Ever since the Suez debacle the British Government had badly needed a major policy coup. In the 1957–58 negotiations with the Six Britain was genuinely anxious to produce a successful European policy providing a fresh role for Britain and a new overseas outlet for her energies and experience, not least her traditional diplomatic apparatus. Yet the evidence (see White Paper, Cmnd 648, January 1959) suggests that the British and the Six were poles apart. Britain was deeply conscious of both her political ties with the Commonwealth and the solid economic benefits which she derived from the association and was not at all anxious to throw them overboard for some vague possible advantages. In essence, the negotiations revealed that Britain wanted freer trade, the Six wanted some form of European unity, though what form of unity remains unclear even now. The ironic point is that at that stage, when Britain assessed the benefits as not worth the price, there was no Common

Agricultural Policy to cope with as there was to be ten years later.

By 1960, the year Britain began to pull out of Africa, the top men in the FO saw Britain's imperial role fading. They saw quite accurately that the Commonwealth could no longer provide a power-base for Britain to play the role of a world power. This came home to them forcibly in the diminished influence British diplomacy seemed to bear in Washington and Moscow. Meanwhile the EEC was being listened to with some care as an emerging world power in its own right, or so it seemed. Although the FO had up until now looked upon the EEC with some grand seigneurial hauteur it now began to see Britain becoming just an offshore island with a rich imperial legacy.

Lord Home (later to become Sir Alec Douglas-Home) was Foreign Secretary at the time, but, possibly more significant for the Common Market issue, Edward Heath became an FO minister in July. After a visit to Washington in March, Macmillan had realized that the Americans thought more highly of the EEC than of EFTA and confidently, if somewhat prematurely looked forward to a strong, united Western Europe. The FO was ready for an about-turn if it would provide a challenging new role and arena to exercise its traditional skills, now of diminishing utility. Macmillan was about to set in motion a crusade whose impetus would last for the next fifteen years at least.

By mid-1960 two of Macmillan's Ministers were Christopher Soames, Minister of Agriculture, and Sir David Ormsby-Gore, Minister of State for Foreign Affairs. As Sir Christopher Soames and Lord Harlech, soon to be British envoys in Paris and Washington respectively, they were to play crucial roles in the ten-year campaign to bring Britain in to the EEC as we shall see both in this and the following chapters. Sir Christopher, son-in-law to Sir Winston Churchill to whom he had been Parliamentary Private Secretary, educated at Eton and Sandhurst, was extrovert, amiable and deceptively able. Like Harlech he thought on the grand scale; neither had any difficulty in subscribing to the concept of the EEC as a great new world power to be governed by supranational institutions. (This may explain Soames' role shortly after his appointment to Paris, which effectively sabotaged De Gaulle's exploratory offer to Harold Wilson of a looser West European grouping.) Harlech, also educated at Eton, went on to New College, Oxford. Imbued with great charm he was a personal friend of John F. Kennedy and subsequently proved a brilliant Macmillan appointment as Ambassador to Washington from 1961 through until 1965. He has been a highly active chairman of the European Movement since 1969. The importance of Lord Harlech and Sir Christopher Soames underlines two features of Britain's entry campaign : first, the central role played by appointed officials and, second, the persisting influence exerted by Washington and Paris.

Meanwhile Macmillan's commitment released the FO for a fresh role and was the greatest single boost to its morale since World War II. The new Community held out the hope not so much of immediate leadership but at least of the prospect of equality with France and West Germany at some not-too-distant date. Though the FO frankly never anticipated that the EEC would effectively "jell", when it began to show signs of success the FO was willing to revise its earlier expectations. It was nonetheless the prospect of a politically united Western Europe rather than an expanded home market which most appealed to the FO. Two key assumptions seem to have dominated the FO's conversion to "Europe".

First, once inside, Britain, thanks to the skill of her diplomatists and higher civil servants, could in all probability become the arbiter of Europe, shaping not only her own but much of Western Europe's future. Second, the supranational element in the Treaty of Rome could be safely ignored wherever and whenever the FO deemed that it seriously infringed on traditional British constitutional rights. There was no reason, in the eyes of the FO, why Britain's essential sovereignity need be impaired. Without challenging such an assumption at this point it may be noted that it reveals an extremely low view of the parliamentary role in the creation of foreign policy. As it turned out under the political imperative of uniting the Labour Party in 1974–75 behind staying in the Community and bringing round those in the country who were agnostic about the Community's claims, renegotiation, both the tactic and the process, had the general effect of fulfilling this FO expectation, at least to a far greater extent than critics of entry might have reasonably expected. The role played by FO and Treasury officials seconded to the EEC Commission in extracting concessions in the renegotiation period should not be underestimated; nor should the efforts of their colleagues in both departments back in Whitehall. None of this, however, would have been possible without a tough negotiating posture and the threat of withdrawal as a very live and concrete option. The fact that British civil servants both within the Commission and in Whitehall were able to exert such influence as they were was due to quite exceptional circumstances. Whether such pressure could be sustained for an indefinite period without Britain permanently souring intra-Community relations and/or threatening the Community's overall cohesion is a question that is far from being answered.

Meanwhile in the early 1960s the rejuvenated FO stood in the wings to some extent, watching helplessly as the first British application began to founder for reasons we have already described in earlier chapters. However, the application was not without its lessons for two of the leading British negotiating figures. Edward Heath, the chief negotiating Minister, learnt that attempting comprehensive and detailed negotiations as a suppliant from outside was fatal to any prospect of success. The differences were unbridgable. Thereafter he determined on entry negotiations based on the very broad principles of the Community (which would have to be accepted), with the detailed negotiations confined to the transitional period only, virtually the entrance fee. Though they greatly enhanced the possibility of entry, even these tactics were not enough until Prime Minister Heath indicated to President Pompidou that he would not adopt a Gaullist stance to protect British interests once membership had been obtained. In other words the possibility of a radical modification of British entry terms was precluded as long as Edward Heath and Georges Pompidou remained at the helm in Britain and France respectively.

The other leading negotiating figure who was profoundly affected by the first application was among the seven key officials named earlier. Sir Eric Roll, a shrewd former professor of economics and commerce at Hull University who was deputy leader of the UK delegation to the EEC from 1961 to 1963, came to much the same conclusions as Edward Heath. With an acute business brain (he is currently chairman of the City merchant bankers, S. G. Warburg), Sir Eric calculated that Britain needed to generate an industrial expansion before attempting entry, both to strengthen her negotiating hand and to take advantage of entry once it had been achieved. Since the Treasury had been the dominating department by custom and since the postwar period had seen a gradual decline in Britain's economic performance compared with her Continental neighbours, Sir Eric was a logical choice to head the new Department of Economic Affairs, conceived by George Brown, Secretary for Economic Affairs (from 1964) and its political boss, as an expansionist rival to the dead hand of Treasury orthodoxy. Whatever the merits of the National Plan that the Department drew up between 1964 and 1966 the sad fact is that by mid-1966 it had been swamped by the torrent of the sterling crisis. Between 1966 and 1968, the period that embraced the second abortive British application to join the EEC, the grim reality was that British economic management had to follow the guidelines laid down by the International Monetary Fund, to which Britain was effectively in pawn. Not unnaturally they demanded a shelving of the great gamble on growth and with it the Department of Economic Affairs lost its impetus if not its *raison d'être*. After a mere two-year interruption the Treasury was once more established as the dominating ministry in British government and the most powerful voice to which the supreme executive body, the Cabinet, had to listen. George Brown, an expansionist by nature, thus thwarted at home, transferred his considerable creative energies to the job he had always coveted, that of Foreign Secretary and almost immediately, in the words of the then Deputy Under Secretary, Sir Denis Greenhill (now Lord Greenhill), "jammed his foot on the accelerator". During his regime the innovation of a special new unit, deceptively blandly called the European Economic Integration Department, provided a concentration of experts who were soon deployed in amassing evidence that would be used to fuel Brown's European crusade within the Cabinet.

By November 1966 when Prime Minister Wilson announced his intention to make a reconnaissance of the Common Market capitals and called for the nation to embark on a "great debate" about entry George Brown's efforts seemed to be beginning to bear fruit. Apart from the underlying reasons of a loss of confidence in the wake of the sterling crisis and constant nudging from the United States to whom Britain was indirectly (through the IMF) heavily in debt, there was a need for a spectacular Wilsonian initiative if the Government was to hold together. There was also the observable phenomenon that while in opposition Harold Wilson's closest political colleagues were largely drawn from Left-wingers such as Richard Crossman, Anthony Wedgwood Benn and Tommy Balogh (later Lord Balogh), in office he of necessity found himself closeted with top civil servants. Among the most influential on the Market issue at this time seem to have been Sir Burke Trend (later Lord Trend), Secretary to the Cabinet Office, and Sir Michael Palliser, whom we have discussed previously. But on Europe one figure stands out clearly above the rest. Sir Con O'Neill. Of the seven key officials who played crucial roles in engineering Britain's entry into the Community his contribution was arguably the most indispensable.

Not only was Sir Con's pedigree for the role he ultimately played impeccable but it almost appeared as if he had known beforehand the role he was eventually going to play. He was born a brother of Terence O'Neill (now Lord O'Neill of the Maine), the aristocratic but liberally disposed former Prime Minister of Northern Ireland whose downfall as a result of pushing reform was to signal the beginning of the contemporary violence in the province. Educated at Eton and Balliol College, Oxford, he was a Fellow of All Souls, Oxford, from 1935 to 1946. After the War he was a leader-writer on *The Times* before joining the Foreign Office, where he served for a period as Head of the News Department and learnt the enormous value of good relations with the national and international press corps. During the first British application he observed from the near touchline, so to speak, as UK Ambassador to Finland. By 1963 he was posted to be Ambassador to the EEC where he gained a very clear idea of the kind of Community that was emerging and with which Britain would have to treat, one way or another. By 1965 he had become Deputy Under Secretary at the FO where he remained until 1968 before falling out with George Brown and leaving to join the City bankers Hill Samuel for a couple of years. He returned to the FO in 1969 and remained until 1972 as leader of the official British delegation charged with negotiating British entry, a charge which manifestly overlapped two very different administrations.

Such an outline does scant justice to his courage, persuasive skill and sheer effectiveness as a committed diplomatist. If De Gaulle's veto had made De Gaulle the FO's most hated man it had been the more galling because Britain's nakedness and impression even of decadence, of not knowing where she was going, was visible to everyone. And national pride is an indispensable element in the *esprit de corps* of a foreign service. Nothing would have been more logical and understandable in human terms than for the FO to shun the EEC, certainly for the rest of De Gaulle's Presidency. During the mid-1960s the role of Sir Con in holding fast Britain's commitment to entry at some future date, both in Brussels and when he returned to Whitehall as Deputy Under Secretary, cannot be overestimated. Certainly he was a major influence in swinging a previously lukewarm Labour Government towards Europe. Indeed, there is little doubt that if the FO had been sceptical of entry it could have swung the Labour Government away from entering the EEC. As early as January 1966 O'Neill presented Michael Stewart, the then Foreign Secretary with a policy paper for presentation to the Cabinet which argued strongly that De Gaulle's conception of a union of fatherlands was unrealistic and inappropriate and that what was required was to strengthen the EEC's already existing supranational bodies. Although this particular paper met with strong opposition from within the Cabinet it represented part of a continuing effort on the part of O'Neill to press for a new British approach as soon as possible.

O'Neill's position at the FO was not only a strong one by virtue of his having spent the previous three years in Brussels but also because he found a willing ally in the Permanent Under Secretary, Lord Gore-Booth. Gore-Booth had returned to Whitehall after five years in India (as UK High Commissioner) only the year before and although he had earned the highest praise for his performance as a deeply humane representative in a highly sensitive diplomatic posting he did not even profess to be deeply conversant with the intricacies of the Common Market issue at this particular stage. It was the kind of situation that gave O'Neill the freedom to take initiatives of his own which were to make him a power to be reckoned with until his temporary departure in 1968. It is possible that without the sympathetic figure of Gore-Booth as his overlord O'Neill's position would have aroused even stronger opposition among the anti-Market Cabinet Ministers than in fact it did, though this lies in the realm of pure speculation. Possibly the fact that Gore-Booth, like O'Neill, was a product of Eton and Balliol helped them to work smoothly together. More likely it was the period that Gore-Booth spent in the United States during the Truman and Eisenhower era that made him receptive to the vision of a United States of Europe.

What can be nailed quite specifically is that O'Neill and his supporters within the FO were ardent supranationalists. Unlike most civil servants who tend to write memoirs in their retirement which are careful to reveal nothing that has not been aired before O'Neill's book *Our European Future* (1972) spells out his supranationalist ideas with some clarity. Among his most loyal lieutenants in his campaign within the FO for British entry was John Robinson, now Ambassador in Algiers. First Secretary to the British delegation to the EEC from 1962 to 1967 and later as Head of the European Economic Integration Department, from 1968 to 1970, Robinson played an essential role as continuity man in the British entry campaign. On O'Neill's recall from private life to conduct the entry negotiations Robinson was a natural choice to join his nine-man negotiating team in Brussels. It is difficult not to admire the dedication and persistence of such unsung heroes of the cause of British entry. Even a critic of both British entry and the growth in the power and range of bureaucracy attendant on it must admit to the presence of a deep integrity allied to the highest professional skills among the British officials rooting for entry.

Setting aside the personalities involved at this point and looking back on the respective roles played by the FO and the Treasury, certain broad conclusions are possible. Ever since 1960, despite some savage setbacks, the FO has been solidly behind British entry and has consistently provided favourable reports, both written and verbal, for the use of successive Conservative and Labour governments alike. But even the FO could not have by itself converted successive administrations to a pro-Europeanist foreign policy without either the support or at least the neutrality of the Treasury. In fact the Treasury on the whole has never been fervently pro-Europeanist, but then neither has it been strongly against. Had it once decided that the price of entry was too high and the benefits too nebulous there is little doubt that such is its commanding position within the Whitehall structure that it could have effectively slowed and ultimately blocked entry whatever protests the FO might have offered. It is against this structural reality that the views of Sir Frank Lee assumed such great importance. For long after his departure from the Treasury, Lee's belief that British industry needed the "cold shower of competition" had become accepted dogma, not so much at the Treasury, who were sceptical about such a simplistic approach, but at the FO. The fact that the FO held such a view throughout the 1960s may partly explain why it has accepted British trade setbacks following British entry with such apparent equanimity and explained them in terms of impact effects which

Britain would eventually overcome. Such a view was certainly believed as the one and only true gospel by the members of the European Economic Integration Department.

Practically parallel in time to Sir Con O'Neill's period as Ambassador to the EEC and later Deputy Under Secretary at the FO was Sir William Armstrong's (later Lord Armstrong) tenure of the post of joint Permanent Under Secretary at the Treasury, that is from 1962 to 1968. Unlike most of the other officials Armstrong became a much more publicly known figure from 1968 to 1974 when he was Permanent Head of the Civil Service. A grammar school boy who went on to Exeter College, Oxford, Armstrong exerted a powerful presence on Treasury policy throughout the mid-1960s. During this period the Treasury view on entry seems to have been that the pros and cons of entry were roughly evenly balanced, though to resume negotiations would be to precipitate a devaluation of sterling. Though the Treasury was to become even more of a brake by the late 1960s and early 1970s under Armstrong's successor, Sir Douglas Allen, scepticism was not enough to overcome those who were heavily committed in favour of entry. By the time that Edward Heath swept to power in 1970 the Civil Service momentum behind Britain's European policy bore all before it. Any doubts that the Treasury may have had about the economic consequences for Britain and its balance of payments were brushed aside by the new Prime Minister who saw any economic price as worth the rich political prizes that might be gained. From this new position Britain could then engage in economic bargaining as an equal member of the Community with Germany and France.

The astounding fact is that after the mid-1960s there does not seem to be a single official document unearthed so far which provides a factual cost-benefit analysis of the effects of entry on the British economy other than the most generalized speculations. The European Liaison group were by this time confined to predicting the consequences of entry rather than debating the alternatives. Thus the White Papers of 1967 and 1971 offer little in the form of evidence likely to convince a professional economist. Faith rather than analysis seems to have provided the basis of much of the Civil Service's conviction that Britain should join the EEC certainly among FO officials who unlike the US State Department were not responsible for the full range of domestic effects. Even the FO's European Economic Integration Department set up in 1966 seems to have subscribed to Sir

Frank Lee's views and not felt it necessary to attempt any serious forecasting of the various alternatives available.

Throughout the three-fold bid for entry, and especially in between those bids, when interest naturally tended to lapse, the FO News Department which briefs the diplomatic correspondents on a daily basis and whose head has usually been a career diplomat rather than a journalist have, unsurprisingly, consistently fed favourable and selected material on the EEC. Since the diplomatic correspondents write much of their material on a non-attributable basis the reports bear the appearance of independent accounts. They may be, but the FO is usually the major if not the sole source.

The assumption to power of Edward Heath in 1970 was all the encouragement that the FO needed to press full steam ahead —as the picking up of the negotiating brief prepared for the Labour Government by their Conservative successors described in the first chapter very clearly indicates. From now until the conclusion of negotiations the FO had the bit between its teeth. An indispensable figure in the final outcome was the last in our group of key officials, Sir Denis Greenhill (later Lord Greenhill). Greenhill, educated at Christchurch, Oxford, had been Minister at the British Embassy in Washington during the period of Lord Harlech's tenure of the Ambassadorship and was thus close to the action during the first application when the Anglo-American rearrangements were so crucial. Unlike Gore-Booth, who had been abroad in the period immediately prior to his assumption of the permanent secretaryship, Greenhill spent the next five years in Whitehall first as Assistant Under Secretary and then as Deputy Under Secretary at the FO. He was thereby fully conversant with the general background to Britain's application and the FO entry strategy in particular when he became Permanent Under Secretary at the FO in 1969.

Like Gore-Booth before him, Greenhill appreciated that the one man who was both personally and technically equipped to carry through any successful application was Sir Con O'Neill. Accordingly Greenhill urged his recall to act as Britain's chief negotiator in the strongest possible terms. This was at a time when the Labour Government with which O'Neill had fallen out was still in office. George Brown, however, had moved on, which made things easier for O'Neill. Greenhill, a shrewd but also benign figure, knew instinctively that O'Neill, with strong political support from Prime Minister Heath as it eventually turned out, knew the Six's attitudes on most questions better than any living British diplomat and that he had the essential will to succeed. In fact, though through no fault of O'Neill's, the negotiations became completely bogged down yet again as the great differences of approach as well as of national interest came to the fore. Once again Greenhill came to the rescue with a behind-the-scenes manoeuvre which was to lead ultimately to a successful conclusion. He saw that the only way through was to settle the issues at the highest political level between the two chief protagonists, namely Britain and France. He and Sir Christopher Soames in Paris, liaising constantly, jointly arranged a "friendly summit" between the British Prime Minister and the French President. The rest is history.

During the period of the Heath Government the Treasury, which up until then had played the role of the sceptic or at least been a brake on accepting too precipitately what might turn out to be adverse terms, was reduced to the role of an onlooker. Thus the 1971 White Paper, which argued entry on the broadest of political fronts, emerged from the Cabinet Office under the control of Sir William Neild rather than from the Treasury. Meanwhile, a new phase of civil service interventionism was being assumed by Sir William Armstrong as with the complete confidence of the Prime Minister he orchestrated Britain's economic strategy, which was to include entry into the Common Market.

While as Lord Greenhill recalls, "We tried to equip ourselves [at the FO] in dealing with the economic as well as the political arguments", it was plainly the political arguments which were beginning to hold sway. "More and more," Lord Greenhill relates. "the entry negotiations involved inter-departmental co-operation". As we have seen, when inter-departmental co-operation is working most closely then is the time when the civil servants are likely to exercise the maximum authority since they, infinitely more than their political masters, tend to be on top of their briefs. The return of a Labour Government in 1974 and the switch to renegotiation was also very much a collabora-tive, inter-departmental effort. Though to begin with the whole exercise was distasteful to very many, particularly at the FO, the process was completed by the latter part of March 1975 under the generalship of Foreign Secretary Callaghan, who earned himself increasing if grudging respect as the renegotia-tions progressed. In a very real sense the FO, and for that matter the British Civil Service as a whole, had shown what it was capable of by coming to grips with a long list of legitimate British interests that needed to be safeguarded. The bureaucracies of the Eight had at last tangled with those of Britain in a realistic series of attempts to reconcile very real national interests. Whether the underlying issues of political sovereignty and parliamentary control had been eroded in the process was a question that the British people would voice their opinion upon around three months later.

THE EUROPEAN LOBBY

By examining in turn each of the two major political parties in Britain and then the Civil Service we have glimpsed the underlying reality of major foreign policy decisions, that once the governmental machine is set on course in a certain direction it acquires a momentum of its own. Nevertheless, since not all political and economic power rests in the hands of the politicians or civil servants there is a need to look at the extra-governmental lobbies whose influence on the debate, or more accurately support for governments' essentially bipartisan orientation towards entry (as distinct from the decision to join), was considerable.

Before examining the European lobby in Britain it is worth making the categoric assertion that the indigenous voluntary lobby, though it called upon financial resources which were at least ten times those pitted against it by the anti-Marketeers, was at all times overshadowed in importance and certainly outspent by the foreign lobbyists. These fall into two categories, those emanating from Brussels which were largely deployed through a single organization, the European Commission Information Services, and those which derived from the United States, which were considerably more diversified, ranging all the way from the US Government itself, through US multinational companies and charitable foundations to, not least, the US Central Intelligence Agency. Since the European Commission Information Services, known as the ECIS, were by far the most consistent propagandists and provided the inspiration and much of the evidence for the US propagandists, they can be usefully considered first.

Without the consistent and skilfully deployed financial support of the ECIS, particularly in the period when General de Gaulle was still in power, the European Movement would have been a hollow exercise. To illustrate the point it is only necessary to reveal that the ECIS spent in the region of £10m from 1960 to 1970 merely to convince important sections of British opinion about the desirability of British entry. Without the regular flow of expenditure on such a scale the European Movement would never have attained the influence it in fact achieved. This is not to say that the ECIS lavished its money around indiscriminately. Far from squandering such sums on mass advertising campaigns designed to persuade the British nation, the Commission's information budget was concentrated on thousands of opinion-formers. While the breakdown of the ECIS budget is deliberately designed to withhold precisely how the money was spent, the ECIS budget in the mid-1960s was running at about £3.5m per annum. (See appendix 19 to the Report of the Select Committee on Agriculture, 66–67, Vol. 2.) Most estimates put the ECIS's expenditure on Britain conservatively at £1m annually throughout most of the 1960s. This figure is made up from direct promotion in Britain, certainly, but a far more important aspect was the expenses paid trip on the EEC circuit provided to thousands of opinion-formers in Britain. Such trips were generally well planned and designed to fit the special interests of the visitor fairly closely. None of this could be regarded as particularly extraordinary if the EEC were merely promoting its image abroad. It is roughly equivalent to the kind of tour arranged constantly by the Central Office of Information and Foreign Office for specialist and official visitors to Britain as a goodwill exercise. But, as the sums spent clearly confirm, the ECIS trips were not mere goodwill trips but exercises in per-suading specific people and interest groups by appealing to their special interests. Financed and directed from outside Britain, with no overall responsibility let alone accountability to the British people, the ECIS, judged by the crudest possible public relations criteria ("Have we promoted a good image abroad of the EEC and minimized its weaknesses?") must rate as an astounding success. By appealing to the self-interest and some-times the idealism of selected individuals the ECIS consistently avoided the disadvantageous aspects of British entry to Britain as a whole.

Some idea of the scope of the ECIS activities may be gleaned from the fact that the EEC budget for public relations rose in 1975 to the colossal figure of £7m annually, a very large pro-portion of which was to be spent by their London, Cardiff and Edinburgh offices. In the 1960s something like one-third of the EEC promotion budget was spent on Britain, so there is no reason to think that during a period when Britain's membership was still in the balance anything less than £2m was being deployed by the ECIS in Britain. Alongside this the Communities' financing of the two British EEC Commissioners, Sir Christopher Soames and George Thomson, in the months prior to the British referendum on membership was a paltry expenditure. On the other hand, by the deployment of two international civil servants, the comprehensive coverage of their every speech in the press, the pro-Marketeers displayed an extraordinary lack of sensitivity to the constitutional ethics of non-interference by international civil servants in the domestic policies of a nation state. In comparing the expenditures of the two contending sides among voluntary groups, the fact that the ECIS was spending such very large sums, in part to pay for propaganda that the voluntary groups then distributed, should not be overlooked. Moreover, the Government's own considerable propaganda material was made available to the voluntary, non-governmental lobbies, particularly during the Heath Administration.

In the spring of 1971, for instance, the Government began to issue a series of eleven "fact-sheets", distributed free of charge from post offices and through mailing lists. These fact-sheets were also widely advertised, the whole operation skilfully implying that the decision had been made (as indeed it had by the administration) and that entry was now no more than a formality. This was followed up on 7 July by the Conservative Government's White Paper. As White Papers go it was stirring-stuff, full or ringing phrases and totally unsubstantiated claims. It was, as Professor Nicholas Kaldor remarked a few days after its publication, "fraudulent" in the sense that any company prospectus which made such claims with no supporting evidence to back them up would be regarded as fraudulent. Not content with a bogus White Paper the Government then issued a sixteen-page free brochure (of which six million copies were printed) showing the much more favourable increase in real income among the Six compared with Britain, though the major argument was that joining the EEC meant greater security for Britain. Most importantly both documents recommended the terms as satisfactory. Together these documents cost the taxpayer around £461,000—this before Parliament had taken note of the terms, let alone voted on their approval. The denigration of Parliament and the erosion of constitutional practice were, by such acts, as apparent in the means of British entry into the EEC as in anything that transpired after entry. As if this were not enough, the Government unleashed a flood (280 to be precise) of ministerial speeches to the press so that during the period between July and October—the most crucial period in so far as the public debate was concerned—there was always a glossy interpretation of events available for public consumption. This was in addition to the disturbingly close links between the media and the European Movement which we shall examine later.

Parallel to the Government machine, for which the majority of Fleet Street was a willing vehicle, the Conservative Central Office and the Conservative Research Department serviced both its MPs and the constituency associates with publications and pamphlets and advisory phone-in services. The Conservative Political Centre was also active in bringing the Conservative faithful to heel. Their services were not in vain, as is underlined by the crucial turn-round in the constituencies from being predominantly anti-Market in the spring to becoming predominantly pro-Market by late summer. It needs re-emphasizing that a majority in favour of entry in the country at large was never achieved in 1971. What mattered to the Government was a parliamentary majority and to achieve this it was necessary to win over the party activists so that the MP could have the feeling that he would not be thrown out when his time came for re-adoption. This limited but entirely necessary objective was convincingly achieved within the Conservative Party. There was also a need for a wider, non-party appeal to the British nation for which a very different kind of organization was required.

As far back as 1955 the UK Council of the European Movement, later to become known as the European Movement, first came into being. Most of its members were either politicians or businessmen, with a sprinkling of visionaries thrown in to leaven the whole.

Among the politicians who were connected with the movement in the 50s were a number who have figured prominently subsequently. They included Geoffrey Rippon, Roy Jenkins and Alfred Robens. The visionaries included Lord Layton, Sir Edward Beddington Behrens, Lord Gladwyn and John Pinder, all of whom have remained totally committed even when their Federalist vision crumbled before the forces of European nationalism. However, it is the composition of the business group in the European Movement which holds the most interest for our purposes since it was they who provided the money when it was needed in the late 1960s to make the big push into Europe. Possibly most significant was the influence which certain leading businessmen were able to exert behind the scenes on both politicians and the media. Viewed collectively the two groups with the greatest influence have been the bankers and the press barons. (In the case of the Cowdray-Lazard nexus, banking and newspaper interests were sweetly combined with the benign influence of Lord Poole thrown in to maintain a close link with the Tory hierarchy.) It is indisputable that both bankers and newspaper magnates were disproportionately over-represented among the ranks of those who actively promoted British entry into the EEC. Among the leading press figures only the Aitken family actively opposed British entry; the great majority of their peers either campaigned vigorously or allowed themselves to be willing vehicles for the official view emanating from either Whitehall or Brussels. The banking fraternity was virtually unanimous. No leading banking group came out against British entry while the great majority of both the joint stock and the merchant banks were strong supporters. The first two treasurers of the European Movement were successively the late Harley Drayton and Sir Kenneth Keith. Drayton had been chairman of the 117 Old Broad Street Group, the leading force in BET, Rediffusion and London, in a word the key man in the introduction of commercial television. He was a notable opponent of nationalization of any sort and by extension of the Labour Party. Sir Kenneth Keith, the chairman of Hill Samuel, was by contrast reputed to be a close adviser to Harold Wilson. He was also believed to be the financial adviser who staunchly resisted countenancing the possibility of devaluation in the period from 1964 to 1966, in hindsight the period most favourable for a devaluation, a policy strongly advocated by the Treasury. To what extent Sir Kenneth influenced Harold Wilson to make his 1967 application to join is a largely unknown factor in the Labour leader's conversion to applying.

The question of what motivated businessmen then and now in favour of joining the EEC is not a straightforward one simply because the business reasons for British entry have changed with time and also because an advantage for some industries is a drawback for others. Among the very earliest spurs to closer ties with Europe was the fear that Britain's manufactures would be excluded from Europe by increasingly high tariff barriers. In spite of the fact that the tariff barriers in industrial goods had, thanks to the Kennedy Round, become relatively insignificant, the Government was still deploying this argument in the late 1960s and early 1970s. Generally speaking, businessmen who wished to export to Europe took a realistic view of the changes taking place and, except where the products they wished to export had only a marginal competitiveness, have taken a sober estimate of the advantages likely to accrue on that score following entry. Later this argument was supplemented and to some extent supplanted by arguments about the stimulation to growth rates of an expanded home market. Apart from the fact that the theoretical evidence to support these arguments is far from proven, such a position fails to make the very important distinction between an industrial free trade area and a traditional home market. In other words, an industrial free trade area has to overcome a host of traditional economic patterns, typically reinforced by a wide variety of non-tariff barriers once the official tariff barriers within the free trade area have been removed.

Nevertheless there have been a number of constant, bedrock reasons so to speak, for much of the support which the business community as a whole has given to British entry. These include first, the widening of business options, the escape from too close a surveillance and control by any single national government and the various restrictions governments impose; third, and finally, the loosening of restraints on capital mobility.

Capital mobility is the overriding reason behind the unanimity of the banking world's and the City establishment's support for the EEC. Ever since 1945 the City has been chafing at Government-imposed restrictions on capital movements, and has been considering means of extending London's already dominating position as a capital market. The EEC's belief in and doctrinal dedication to a totally free movement of all factors of production was the sweetest sound the City had heard since the end of the war. As the European idealists dream of democratic federations, so the City sees all major capital transfers within the Community being channelled through London banks and brokers. Other service industries such as insurance and advertising to some extent share this dream though with less justification since their expansion has already caused restrictive measures to be discussed in Brussels.

On the face of it not only the City but most of Britain's best-known international companies (including those which were either partially or predominantly American owned) supported British entry in the belief that they stood to benefit from the enlarged market. Thus among the corporate subscribers to the European Movement have been such famous names as ICI, ICL, IBM, Honeywell, Dunlop, Caterpillar, BP, Esso, Reckitt & Colman, Metal Box, Morgan Crucible, Kodak, Singer and many more. Even major companies which have held back from contributing directly to the European Movement have independently abetted the same cause by placing major advertisements, often worth thousands of pounds, in the national press expressing their confidence at the thought of European competition. Not insignificantly they have included Lord Stokes of Leyland, Britain's largest car manufacturer and exporter, and Sir Ray Brookes of GKN. By 1973 Lord Stokes was speaking out in favour of restricting the Japanese in Europe as the continental car salesmen began to bite deep into the British home market. Sir Ray Brookes has diplomatically kept silent as Britain moved towards a deficit of around £1,000m with the EEC in the first year of entry, 1973, and a more than £2,000m non-oil deficit in 1974.

The sometimes explicit, sometimes implicit argument that what was good for X company was good for Britain was widely and plausibly deployed in the promotion campaign and was reinforced by the sheer weight of numbers. How could anything which was so obviously attractive to such a large number, indeed the majority of major companies, it seemed, be anything but beneficial for British industry and thus the British work force, British investors and the British nation as a whole? To some considerable extent it was believed by the men who headed many of the major companies. It was undoubtedly what they hoped to achieve. However, there were other factors, rarely emphasized, but no less important for all that, which may help to put British business calculations into a broader perspective.

Virtually all the corporate subscribers to the European Movement just mentioned have productive capacity located somewhere within the original Six as well as in Britain. Many of them of course have had this capacity for many years; some have acquired it only recently when it was becoming increasingly probable that Britain would join the EEC. Most of them are expanding their European capacity. To give only the most notable examples ICI is increasing its chemical complex in the Netherlands and in France (a major plant near Marseilles);

there is the Dunlop-Pirelli tie-up, which despite its disastrous early effects remains an area of future expansion for Dunlop; GKN and Morgan Crucible have each acquired plants in Germany, and so on. Yet the argument runs, and is generally accepted, that economies of scale derive from centralizing production rather than dispersing it. One might well ask why then are British firms with considerable British plants so eager to buy into alternative locations?

The answer is fairly straightforward and arises from fairly similar expectations of British entry to those held by the City. With Britain a member of the EEC, the argument runs, a free flow of resources between Britain and Europe will be possible. In consequence firms will be free to invest in those areas where production will be most profitable. As long as Britain remains separate from the EEC, the argument continues, British firms are obliged to concentrate their production in Britain both to serve the British market and because Bank of England permission is required to export the capital to expand abroad. With Britain inside the EEC both restraints are removed. In the case of US giants like Ford only the first restraint applied, though both Ford and Chrysler certainly favoured British entry. Following entry British and US firms automatically achieved a significant extension of what are politely called policy options. These policy options strengthen the hand of the big companies in their bargaining with either labour or government by the implicit threat of taking their capital elsewhere. Thus, if the rate of inflation in Britain reaches an unacceptable level, or if the weakness in the balance of payments forces the Government to institute even higher interest rates and eventually siege economy measures, it will be of paramount interest to Britain how the bankers and businessmen who have backed British entry react. There is not much doubt that they will transfer substantial capital and plant to the Continent. During 1973, the first year of British membership of the EEC, investment by British companies into her Continental partners was seven times that of European companies into Britain, a trend which is likely to accelerate as time goes on.

Until General de Gaulle retired from the political scene, almost the entire cost of promoting the pro-Market campaign in Britain was borne by the European Commission Information Services. With the General out of the way, the various European pressure groups saw that the time was ripe to merge under the banner of the European Movement. The prospect of entry was no longer blocked by an inflexible French President and the possibility of spending money to some purpose was an added incentive to the business community to contribute funds on a substantial scale. The Labour Government, incidentally, provided £7,500 annually throughout its period in office towards the costs of the European Movement.

By 1971 the European Movement's budget was in the vicinity of £500,000 and for the very first time in the ten-year campaign the general public were appealed to directly in a national press campaign (to have been augmented by television advertising had the ITA not banned it). In fact in the first seven months of 1971 the European Movement spent more than £40,000 on press advertisements. So much for the general rationale and motivation which lay behind the substantial support for the European Movement from big business. It remains to describe the manner in which the funds were deployed and how the European Movement's campaign developed.

Although the British Council of the European Movement as such was not formed until 1969 it had grown out of a cluster of organizations that had grown up since the late 1940s. Among these were the UK Council of the European Movement whose president was a City financier, Sir Edward Beddington Behrens, a close friend of Harold Macmillan. As early as 1960 the UK Council was running conferences and publishing a glossy magazine in a thoroughly well financed exercise which was to typify the subsequent history of the later European Movement. The other principal body which was to pool forces with Sir Edward's organization in 1969 was the Britain in Europe Group, a much younger, more politically committed group, whose predominant vision was of a federalist Western Europe. This was no accident since a large number of the Britain in Europe Group had benefited from the creation of the Federal Trust for Education and Research which since 1945 had concentrated on research to promote European unity—a task which it continues to sponsor by research projects and conferences, etc. From these two groups, and particularly the latter, Britain in Europe, were to come some of the chief figures not only of the European Movement but of the whole intricately orchestrated campaign to bring Britain into the EEC. The interlocking nature of British big business with the European Movement is illustrated in the origins of Britain in Europe which essentially grew out of a study produced by the Economist Intelligence Unit published in 1957 under that name. The role of the *Economist* newspaper itself was to be crucial later in the moulding of business opinion towards the view that entry would be virtually uniformly beneficial to British industry.

Meanwhile the 1963 veto had dealt a considerable blow to the morale of Britain in Europe. It was nonetheless able to survive, sustained in large part by the ongoing task and resources of the Federal Trust which maintained its programme of conferences and dinners. In 1967, the crisis had passed and a further British application was on the table. At Britain in Europe, now ten years of age, Ernest Wistrich took over as Director to lead a fresh offensive. Very soon they embarked on a major fundraising campaign, kicking off with a dinner presided over by Lord Gladwyn at which the future French President, Giscard D'Estaing, was the guest of honour. It raised about £20,000. The Group held its most lucrative dinner, however, in July 1969 at the Guildhall (attended by both the Prime Minister and the Leader of the Opposition) when £450,000 was pledged in tax-exempt seven-year covenants to the European Educational Research Trust. By the beginning of 1970 the Britain in Europe Group had staged a virtual takeover of the UK Council of the European Movement to create the new European Movement. It was effectively the combining of a politically virile group of activists, in the shape of Britain in Europe, with that of an Establishment shell which gave the air of respectability essential to the fund-raising campaign ahead.

Before the Labour Government went down to defeat at the polls in 1970, when the forecasters were almost unanimous in assuming a Labour victory, the new European Movement was already discussing with Labour Ministers how they could collaborate with the Government's third attempt at entry. Although the Movement claimed to be strictly neutral as between the parties nobody could doubt that the election of Edward Heath at the head of the majority party was an unexpected boost to the Movement's morale. It was a great comfort to know that the new Prime Minister would do all he could to aid the Movement since its chief aim only reinforced his own long cherished ambition to take Britain into the EEC.

The campaign of the European Movement as it unfolded during the Heath administration was to reveal aspects reminiscent of the 1968 election of US President Richard Nixon in its attempt to blanket the media with a uniformly favourable impression of the EEC and Britain's prospects within it. One of the more obvious differences between the two was the greater independence shown by the major US newspapers as compared with the British press. The reasons for this are not hard to find and are more institutional and procedural than personal, though the personal aspect cannot be divorced from the pattern of propaganda which was turned on the British people from 1970 through until 1975. The campaign methods about to be described have the utmost relevance to the referendum held in mid-1975 if only because they reveal the extraordinary length and intensity of the public relations effort put out by the pro-Europeanists, in which nothing was left to chance.

The starting point of the European Movement when Edward Heath came to power in 1970 was that they already possessed the commanding heights of the British propaganda system. That is, they knew they could count on the wholehearted support not only of the new Government but of the Whitehall machine as well as that of the ECIS. The most obvious requirement was to co-ordinate the Government's forces with her allies in all three parties as well as in the European Movement, and not least within the media. To meet this challenge, the European Movement established what it called the Campaign Group, an inter-party committee to oversee its own activities. This was in turn complemented by the Government's Co-operation Group which was designed to smooth communications and avoid duplication between the Government and the Movement. Finally, there were what became known unofficially (since they were more or less secret) as "media breakfasts"—whose purpose was to provide the media with all the necessary information to make the campaign run freely. Each of these three groups had an overlapping membership which served to promote their general objective. Many of the key members of these groups regarded what was taking place as an object example in citizen participation in the democratic process and the pursuit of a certain foreign policy in particular. The trouble with this view is that it overlooked the fact that there was no guarantee of a parliamentary majority in favour of this policy; it had never been clearly put to the electorate; and that civil servants who were constitutionally impartial were participating in a campaign very much behind the public's back, certainly without the public's knowledge (the press were hardly likely to admit they were being hand-fed on such a controversial and nationally divisive issue). The degree of embarrassment, possibly even a trace of guilt, about the violation of constitutional niceties was apparent in the fact that a civil servant who regularly attended the Campaign Group was recorded in the minutes of one meeting, leading to the hasty issue of an urgent directive to remove his name. As we have seen in the chapter on the Civil Service it was not until after Britain's accession in January 1973, when the European unit of the Cabinet Office was created, that any inter-departmental body was acknowledged as existing to co-ordinate Government policy on the issue. To this extent the *ad hoc* committees just described were an almost inevitable out-growth of the Government's commitment to obtain entry. It was clearly deemed indiscreet to formalize these groups, which nonetheless had the clearest of official sanctions and encourage-ment from No. 10.

It was apparent from experience, during World War II in particular, that there was an inbuilt resistance to purely govern-ment information services which could only achieve so much and which needed to be supplemented by less professionally committed sources. Thus it was a considerable advantage to the pro-Marketeers to have a vigorous, voluntary, and ostensibly non-governmental auxiliary to the Government.

Within the Government itself the minister charged with responsibility for the Government's propaganda campaign, William Whitelaw, was also Leader of the House of Commons. It was a very shrewd joint appointment since Whitelaw, apart from his outstanding personal qualities of warmth and good humour, had a rare capacity to make people from very different viewpoints pull together. Thus the earliest meetings to plan the co-ordination of the European Movement, the media and the Government often took place in Whitelaw's personal office. Six months after, when the campaign had gathered momentum, the co-ordinating group met at the Foreign Office. This later com-mittee was presided over by the Parliamentary Under Secretary of State at the Foreign Office, Anthony Royle. By November 1970, this group of civil servants and their voluntary associates were disbanded with a letter of thanks from the Prime Minister. They had worked admirably in sharing their ideas and ensuring that the auxiliary campaign felt itself part of the Government exercise. In its turn the European Movement provided the Government with reports on opinion polls which it had commissioned.

The most obvious problem within these three co-ordinating bodies was to prevent a battle between the two major parties breaking out. Thus when the Labour Party began to respond to feelings in the grass roots and swing away from entry, the Labour sympathizers in those committees were adamant in insisting that to attack Labour too emphatically would be counter-productive in that it would confirm the suspicions in the country that the Government did not care very much what the grass roots felt about British entry. This did not prevent a campaign of vilification and innuendo at the expense of the Leader of the Opposition that needs to be viewed within the wider context of the role of Fleet Street, a task outside the scope of this particular book. If, as they claim, the co-ordinating group acted as a brake on press criticism of the Labour leader, that is an implicit criticism of the level of commitment of Fleet Street generally and their total inability to draw a distinction between a commitment to entry and a commitment to negotiate, not an especially subtle distinction to grasp, but one which most of the quality newspapers and editorials steadfastly ignored. One cannot escape the conclusion that the Fleet Street editors and particularly sub-editors concerned comprehended well enough, but were angry that a major party leader could modify his position in response to the manifold expression of opinion from within his party and in the country at large. The commitment of Fleet Street editors in many cases exceeded that of many pro-Marketeer MPs and differed appreciably from the parliamentarians in that they could hold these views without any obligation to listen to the hopes and fears of the people in the constituencies.

Thus when the European Movement staged its media breakfasts at the ritzy Connaught Hotel it was more as a response to requests from the media than from any Government plot to seduce them—they were only too willing. The breakfasts, the brainchild of a public relations consultant, Geoffrey Tucker, who had been the Conservative Party's publicity director, were also greatly helped by Jim Garrett who, like Tucker, had masterminded the Conservative Party 1970 political programmes on television. Tucker, a member of the Conservative Group for Europe, chaired the media breakfasts which were also attended by Ministers and civil servants, where the theme that would dominate Fleet Street that week would be openly discussed. Unlike a press conference, which usually has the implication of two opposing parties, one of the chief functions of these Connaught breakfasts was to let the Government and especially Whitehall know what was required if the public relations campaign was to be successful. Thus these meetings were not only important to the media men who attended, but not least to the Government officials. For behind any government in Britain stands an army of information officers to explain the policies of each major department, not to mention the Central Office of Information whose role is to provide a propaganda back-up for all major government policies, not least to governments and news services abroad. Such is the dedication to propaganda of some of these officers that a Ceylonese desk man at the COI overly sensitive to the feelings of Indian cricket enthusiasts, once wrote a description of a test match between India and England in which he hid the fact that India were annihilated in an innings defeat! Somewhat more seriously, the media breakfasts provided an invaluable means of easy communication between the Government and their allies within the media. When Treasury officials revealed that in concrete terms the prospects following entry might not be as easy as had been supposed, they were quickly replaced by City editors whose commitment to entry was less hedged with doubts about the effects on the British economy as a whole.

How effective this campaign proved to be with the British public is difficult to assess—its effectiveness obviously varied. On the one hand quality weeklies like the *Sunday Times, Observer* and *Economist* were enthusiastically co-operative although their less well-heeled fellow weeklies like the *New Statesman* and the *Spectator* never quite bought the pro-Market line, indeed remained consistently critical. On the other hand the quality dailies were in support of the pro-Market campaign without exception. Indeed only the Beaverbrook press stood out against this torrent of words in favour of entry. But the major target of the media breakfast was the mass circulation dailies, television and radio. Here they had their greatest success in putting over the pro-Market view to a multi-million audience.

Independent Television News, with a viewing audience of up to fifteen million at times, was a crucial outlet on which a five-minute slot on the Common Market appeared after the main weekday bulletin almost throughout July, the most crucial month in terms of the media campaign. The BBC radio news magazine programme *Today* also provided daily morning reports from Brussels on the negotiations. How effective these and the support of mass dailies like the *Mirror* and *Sun* were to the pro-Market cause has yet to be properly assessed.

Meanwhile, the European Movement's Campaign Group was equally busily deployed in its own exercise in persuasion directed by Ernest Wistrich from Chandos House, Victoria. In fact the European Movement was an umbrella for around a dozen pro-Market organizations, each with their own professional staff and voluntary supporters. But the Movement was far from being an amateur organization left out in the cold. For a start, its weekly Campaign Group meetings were attended by a member of the Foreign Office staff, an example of many links between the pro-Market organizations and the Government during 1971. Secondly, in the period from November 1970 to November 1971, when it was disbanded, the Group employed in excess of fifty people (including a dozen regional organizers). Thirdly, its campaign of persuasion was directed at convincing opinion-formers rather than engaging in open debate. One of the main reasons was that the arguments deployed in favour of entry were tailored to fit particular people and thus differed widely where they did not flatly contradict earlier arguments.

To the extent that it was a mixture of professionals and amateurs working together, the European Movement was a strange mixture of skilful professional PR and amateur enthusiasm. Among its professional advisers were the PR firm of Collett, Dickinson, Pearce and Partners, retained for £1,500 per month; Norman Hart of Gywnne Hart & Associates, for promotion among the Labour Movement; and Roland Freeman of Freeman & Garlich who promoted the activities of the Conservative Group for Europe Committee as well as participating in the Campaign Group. In addition there were PR firms advising each of the Northern England, Scottish and Yorkshire regional groups of the European Movement. As a direct consequence of the professional advice they were receiving, the European Movement deployed all the available techniques of modern marketing. This included the conducting of selected surveys which helped them to discern what the public was thinking and especially what it was most concerned about. An added bonus was that it also enabled them, when the material gathered looked favourable, to have it published. Both Social and Community Planning Research Ltd and the Opinion Research Centre were regularly employed to conduct surveys and polls.

The most recurrent themes in the questionnaires which were put out were that British entry was by implication in the national interest and that it would benefit future generations. Since neither assertion lent itself to proof the Movement was on safe enough ground. However, questions like "if the negotiations are successful [the terms being unspecified and unknown by anyone other than the negotiators and their governments], would you accept the terms negotiated by the Government?" and "Do you think that the present negotiations will be successful?" were obviously to be used for propaganda purposes thus : X per cent of the population polled are in favour of accepting the Government's terms; and X per cent of the population polled believe the negotiations will be successful—all good propaganda if completely meaningless. Another poll showed the better-informed to be more favourable to entry, not mentioning the fact that 90 per cent of the material available to them (provided by either the Government or commercial media) was predicated in favour of entry and that the European Movement's own campaign had been heavily concentrated on the better-informed and opinion-makers. But this was just the feedback from the promotion campaign proper.

As early as January 1971 the SCPR pilot survey had nailed the fact that the campaign must satisfy both personal material needs and abstract ideals and allow everyone to play out whatever role he or she saw as important for themselves and for Britain—all of which was only attainable from within the EEC. The outcome of entry for each of them must be presented as something known and concrete. As a result of this and other surveys the campaign set itself to promote five leading themes; higher standards of living, better social welfare, strength through unity, protection of national interests through participation in European decisions, and Britain's world role. Three months later when the negotiations had become bogged down and some of the earlier goals had become plainly unattainable the themes were modified to stress social security, the strengthening of trade-union links and peace and security arrangements. The second SCPR report had revealed that the people polled were not entirely sold on the vision of the marvellous opportunities for higher standards of living but were in fact somewhat fearful. Such a view would explain both the modification of the campaign theme and fit the general theory of this book that Britain's primary underlying motivation to join the EEC on the part of the leadership of both major political parties was fundamentally based on a fear that Britain could no longer manage her national affairs alone. The emphasis had to be that entry would both solve Britain's economic problems and restore Britain's influence and prestige in world affairs. By May the campaign also began to stress the material benefits to be gained by comparing the wage packets of British and of EEC workers (while studiously ignoring prices).

The dollar crisis of August 1971 was a great boon to the Movement's campaign and was offered as a warning of the vulnerability of Britain in any trade war that might develop (without specifying too precisely how joining the EEC would protect British interests) and of how political and economic power was now shifting from the United States to Europe. Again responding to events in the shape of increased unemployment, the campaign stressed the alleged industrial advantages of entry which would, they claimed, boost industrial expansion. (Had not the Prime Minister equated entry with economic and industrial expansion and so decreed it to his Treasury and Cabinet Office officials?) And to calm the fears of the North, Scotland and Wales there was a sticker campaign in August asserting: "For more jobs in Britain—say Yes to Europe." Among officials of the Commission in Brussels charged with promoting EEC regional and industrial policies there was some disquiet that such claims were not capable of fulfilment except in terms of isolated cases. All the evidence of the previous history of the Six showed that the growth points were almost entirely in the central areas of the Community.

Altogether during the financial year 1971–2 something of the order of £250,000 was spent on public relations and advertising, the largest single category of expenditure. The advertising campaign was therefore, financially speaking, the most important aspect of the campaign. It was accordingly planned with considerable care and forethought. The original intention was to have a three-phase plan comprising first, up to July, a wide dissemination of facts in the newspapers; second, from the announcement of the terms until the end of the party conferences, a national poster campaign; and thirdly, a concentrated effort on the constituencies of marginal MPs—marginal in the sense that they could be influenced. By the end of April however, as the prospects in the constituencies were rather bleak for the pro-Marketeers, it was decided to run the constituency phase alongside the national campaigns. During July, by general consent the climax of the public debate, the European Movement held around 4,000 meetings attended by around 100,000 people. It also distributed vast quantities of literature from door to door. Yet, and this is an important point, despite its connections with the Establishment in government, in industry, in the media, etc., compared with its opponents in the Safeguards Campaign, for instance, it never became an effective grass-roots movement. The classic illustration of this very basic difference between the contending sides is seen in the relative failure of this impressively organized and lavishly backed movement when it attempted forays at the grass roots. In September, the Movement sent out 290,000 pre-paid postcards expressing support for entry to be returned signed to Chandos House for forwarding to the constituent's MP. It was a well-conceived piece of persuasion attempting some direct grass-roots pressure on the men and women on whom the decision about entry now essentially rested. By mid-October, however, only 6,000 of these postcards had been returned and even if 4,000 more came in after the October issue of the Campaign's tabloid had carried a foldable version, 10,000 signatures was a somewhat unfavourable contrast with the Safeguards' Petition containing 600,000 signatures! It is indeed not difficult to discern in the European Movement the outlines of an élitist clique sincere, gifted, often idealistic and as often self-motivated, but above all else, well-backed. Little wonder that it has steadfastly resisted the idea of a referendum. Its arguments against the use of a referendum have been many but always one suspects that under the cloak of defending the supremacy of Parliament there is the awkward self-knowledge that yes, they *are* élitists and that the people will never be able to tell what is good for them. In what other long-established democracy, one might ask, in the face of the most drastic changes in the Constitution, would a body of people seriously argue that a referendum was undesirable? Would the Canadian Parliament pass an Act of Union with the United States without submitting such a step to the direct verdict of the Canadian people? It is unthinkable; yet the United States and Canada have a far more closely integrated political, economic and cultural tradition than have Britain and the Eight (especially the Six). Yet during 1971 the European Movement verged on the hysterical in its attacks on proposals for a referendum. "Referendum Madness" screamed the Movement's tabloid, the *British European,* which incidentally sometimes had print runs of up to 1.5 million copies. It went on to argue the folly of a referendum when the public was so widely ignorant. While admitting the ignorance, the answer is that had the Government wished to tell the unselected facts during the previous ten years the public would be far better informed and probably, as the European Movement very likely knew, even less keen about entry. Indeed, as an opinion survey commissioned by the Movement embarrassingly revealed, although 80 per cent felt they were not well enough informed to vote in a referendum (a reasonable position before entry, though not quite as powerful an argument post entry), of those who felt at all strongly about the Common Market, more were strongly against than strongly in favour. A referendum, as the Movement then realized, was not the sort of instrument that élitist movements can readily manipulate. From that day to this the European Movement has opposed referenda on general grounds of "principle".

By the summer and autumn of 1971 the Government and Conservative Party machines had, as we have already described, been brought fully into play. The European Movement had to find for itself a supporting role where previously it had played a general softening-up role. It fixed on the job of rallying the grass-roots activists who were in favour of entry, not least to stiffen the resolution of the wavering pro-Market MPs, but also one suspects to dispose of its image of high-flown élitism. The results, unfortunately, were not especially convincing. There are few things less dignified than an élitist pretending to be one of the boys. To give him his due Roy Jenkins for one never stooped to such "razmataz". But elements in the European Movement obviously felt the need to prove that they were a popular movement in tune with the spirit and more especially the promotional methods of the time.

Breezy ads appeared in the mass circulation dailies and Sundays urging readers to say "Yes to Europe"; the same slogan was carried on household goods ranging from tea towels to carrier bags and even balloons. All this was pretty harmless fun. A more sinister note crept in when the Movement advertised the fact that they had insured a flashing light panel quiz at the Daily Mail Ideal Home Exhibition, held at Olympia, against "attacks by Right-wing extremist elements". It was one of those gratuitous slurs against their opponents which the Movement's leaders were embarrassed about but did nothing to suppress. Indeed it was an important and highly successful aspect of the Movement's image-building efforts that the anti-Marketeers should be depicted as extremists, out of touch with informed opinion, etc. Interestingly enough British economists seem to have been about equally divided about the benefits accruing or not accruing from entry, though the critics seemed to have retained the support of the most illustrious names such as Professor Nicholas Kaldor (now Lord Kaldor) and Professor James Meade at Cambridge, Sir Roy Harrod, Lord Balogh and Peter Oppenheimer at Oxford and Professor Harry Johnson, Professor Allan Walters and Edward Mishan at the London School of Economics, representing the very widest spectrum of economic philosophies.

Meanwhile in mid-summer the Movement pressed ahead with its subliminal campaign to portray entry as being part of the inevitable march of progress—mostly in the shape of about $6\frac{1}{2}$ million pieces of literature designed for everyone from housewives to borough councillors. The flagship of this "literacy on Europe" campaign was the *British European*, a monthly tabloid distributed free that grew from 20,000 copies in January to 1,500,000 copies in the July-August holiday edition. If the *British European* and its arguments are to be taken at face value then British entry is a good thing because such swinging figures of the 60s as Mary Quant, Petula Clark, Bobby Moore and Kenneth More recommend it. This is not quite as innocent an argument as one might suppose. As the advertising man will tell you, identification of the reader with the product is half the battle and many of the readers of *British European* were known to identify with one, or some, if not all the celebrities listed.

Among the more disturbing aspects of the Movement's summer promotion campaign was its treatment of its own opinion polls. The overriding concern of the British people which these polls revealed was that entry would involve a loss of control over Britain's national future, i.e. the question of sovereignty. This crucial fact was deliberately minimized in their accounts of the survey given to the press, which stressed the economic arguments and misled the anti-Marketeers into concentrating on the economic issues on which the people were convinced entry would mean a definite gain. So much for the actual campaign sustained by the European Movement which was largely concentrated during the spring and summer months of 1971. Both in the scope and quality of the professional services they deployed as well as the range and quantity of their activities the anti-Marketeers had no answer to the European Movement and its allies in government (both at home and abroad) and big business (also both at home and abroad). It was simply a case of the professionals versus the amateurs. But a professional campaign, admittedly supported by considerable voluntary effort, clearly requires a great deal of money. The question that needs to be answered is where did that money come from?

The original plan of the European Movement was to have a two-year campaign running to not more than £500,000 of which about half would be devoted to advertising and publications. The next largest allocation, of about £50,000 was to be for cash grants to friendly bodies. But in the single financial year 1971-2 alone the Movement spent around £550,000. This reflected both the need to win over supporters in the constituencies and the consequently high level of activity of the Movement throughout 1971. The anti-Marketeers, by contrast, though equally active, deployed probably less than £50,000 all told throughout the same period. The short answer to where did the Movement's money come from is that in 1971-2 £900,000 of it came from subscriptions and donations, and only a relatively minor allocation from the Government. The breakdown of these donations is most revealing. As the Director of the Movement, Ernest Wistrich, repeatedly stated, "Both in amount and number of donations and subscriptions to the Movement, individuals outnumber companies considerably." This seems to have been true, though the contribution of several major British companies for reasons we have already examined was not inconsiderable. They included, first, the big banks, Barclays, Lloyds and National Westminster and most of Britain's biggest companies, BAT, BEA, BET, BP, British Ropes, Courtaulds, Distillers, Dunlop, Imperial Tobacco, ICL, Laporte Industries, J. Lyons, Marks & Spencer, Metal Box, Morgan Crucible, Reckitt & Colman, Shell, W. H. Smith and Watney Mann. Also well represented were the US multinational companies Caterpillar Tractor, Esso, Heinz, Honeywell, IBM, Kelloggs, Kodak, Singer and Woolworths.

There is a general calculation that something like £800,000 came from two or three officially anonymous private individuals. Whether any one of these was in fact a front for a large foreign organization has been the subject of considerable debate which does not yet lend itself subject to proof. The denials by the CIA have been in the nature of an organization, which, while admitting a long-term interest in promoting the security of the United States in Europe by aiding British entry into the EEC, is pained at being suspected of deploying money in Europe in the same way as it has in Latin America. The trouble is that it became public knowledge some years ago that the CIA was subsidizing the literary politico-cultural journal *Encounter*, a notably enthusiastic early advocate of British entry, and the suspicion remains that as the entry campaign expanded so did the CIA's financial involvement. As in Chile, when the protection of the interests of ITT and other US companies figured prominently in the reasons behind the CIA's active involvement, the stake held by US companies in British industry is considerable. Their reasons for wishing to have Britain within the Community are basically no different from those of comparably sized British companies : the greater degree of business options open to them in the deployment of both capital and labour. Indeed in a front page article in *The Times* of February 1975, the writer Peter Hennessy reported that "at least five American-based multinational corporations are believed to have informed the Government that they are holding up investment plans in the United Kingdom until the result of the referendum is known". The veracity of this report, although no companies are named, need not be seriously questioned. It has always been in the interests of US multinationals to have Britain in the EEC as the growth of US companies in Europe since 1958 demonstrates. It is a truism to say that US business is the major economic beneficiary of the establishment of the EEC, and, by the same coin, of its enlargement to include Britain, Ireland and Denmark. Where the long-term political and strategic objectives of the US Government coincide with that of the majority of US multinational companies it would be unreasonable not to expect the active support and participation of the CIA. The goal of the unity of Europe has been as much an American vision as it has been of a minority of European statesmen, as our final chapter cumulatively underscores.

As a result of this ample funding in 1971–2, the European Movement ended a year of active campaigning with a surplus of £200,000. To demonstrate its gratitude and continuing need for the Movement's support the Government promptly increased the Movement's grant from £7,500 to £20,000. Meanwhile the

Movement was skilfully extracting the maximum financial advantage out of its income by a very close partnership with the European Educational and Research Trust whose main role was to educate and inform the 18–38 age-group about the EEC. By virtue of being a charitable trust the EERT was free of income and corporation tax. Not only did it share the same premises and staff with the European Movement but three of its Council of Management were officers of the European Movement.

That the European lobby played an important part in the passage of the European Communities Bill through Parliament would be a fair conclusion. Whether they succeeded in winning over the mass support of the British people is open to serious doubt. Nevertheless, to many of the bureaucrats in Whitehall and in Brussels (not to mention Washington and Paris), the decisions having been made, the value of the lobbyists was to involve Britons and to make them believe they were doing the persuading, as indeed to some extent they were. Where such campaigns succeed or fail—whether in the corridors of power or the market place of ideas—is something to be taken up in the Conclusion.

V

THE ANGLO-AMERICAN CONNECTION

"Great Britain has lost an empire and has not yet found a role. The attempt to play a separate power role, that is a role apart from Europe, a role based on a 'special relationship' with the United States, a role based on being the head of a 'commonwealth' which has no political structure, or unity, or strength and enjoys a fragile and precarious economic relationship by means of the sterling area and preferences in the British market—this role is about played out."

THE VERY FAMILIARITY of these words uttered by an urbane and erect former US Secretary of State in a speech on European union at the US Military Academy, West Point, on a cold December day in 1962 has tended to obscure their true significance. For Dean Acheson, product of Groton School, Yale University and Harvard Law School, an archetypal representative of the Eastern Establishment, had just fired the opening salvo in the ten-year American campaign to edge Britain into the European Economic Community. He had also articulated, with a breadth of candour which only elder statesmen are allowed, the principles which had underlain US foreign policy towards Britain for the previous thirty years, and which Acheson had himself played a not insignificant part in implanting, especially in the immediate postwar period. Flushed with the dazzling diplomatic triumph of President John F. Kennedy in the Cuban missile confrontation with Soviet Premier Nikita Krushchev, Acheson judged the moment opportune to come clean about where America's national interests lay. As a senior adviser to the young President his speech can be assumed to reflect the President's own views; certainly they were never publicly disowned by the then incumbent of the White House.

That Acheson should be attacking the same old canards of Commonwealth preferences and sterling thirty years after the US State Department first took up the cudgels against them is at least evidence of their resilience in the face of consistent US hostility. Ten years before Acheson's West Point speech the then US Under Secretary of State, Mr Sumner Welles, had said, "the whole history of British Empire Preference is a history of economic aggression". The truth is, if history must be invoked, that by the end of the last war the extended isolation of the United States from the full impact of external economic forces, together with its astonishing internal growth, had created a mood of confidence in the virtues of free trade comparable to that which Britain herself experienced in 1845, which similarly ushered in a thirty-year period of economic expansion and general prosperity. Such was the strength of American attachment to the principles of free trade in general and the principle of most favoured nation treatment in particular, i.e. non-discrimination, that it failed to discern that the British preference system was among the most liberal and least discriminatory then devised, hence its durability and the survival of its essential principles in the European Free Trade Association which correspondingly benefited its members and harmed nobody. The real roots of the antagonism towards imperial and later Commonwealth preferences rested on the idealistic grounds that imperialism and its surviving legacy was by definition bad and the practical grounds that such preferences reduced the scope of American economic expansion.

Accordingly in 1933, at the London Economic Conference, hard on the heels of the Ottawa Conference of the previous year which had drawn up Empire preferences which were to lift its members out of the slump more effectively than any comparable group of nations, the cause of multilateral tariff reduction and preference abolition was fulsomely argued. However, no agreement was reached since the continental gold countries demanded a prior settlement of the monetary problem, foreshadowing a set of national alignments on these very same issues which was to recur again and again right up into the 1970s. In the same year President Roosevelt reduced the dollar to 50 per cent of its previous gold value, prior to government purchase, a step which led to the resignation of the firmly internationalist then Under Secretary of the Treasury, Dean Acheson.

Only weeks after the Munich Agreement of 1938 an Anglo-American Trade Agreement was signed circumscribing Empire preferences to the extent that government monopolies were forbidden from concluding reciprocal terms with Empire countries. Less specific, but of greater long-term significance, was the acceptance by the British Government of the principle of the most favoured nation clause. The outbreak of war gave the US State Department a golden opportunity to pursue its policies with increasing vigour given that Britain was cast in the role of a suppliant for both arms and credit. The American position was stated succinctly by Mr Sumner Welles in a memorandum to M Paul Reynaud on 9 March 1940 setting out "The base of the economic foreign policy of the United States" as, in effect, getting rid of all bilateralism or discriminatory arrangements in favour of the implementation of the most favoured nation clause, and of excessive tariffs, quantitative regulating and exchange controls in favour of "the multilateral functioning of the trade process". Most of these objectives would be accepted as desirable today, but that they were seen as primary goals of US foreign policy at a time when Britain was fighting for survival is grimly revealing. If there was any lingering doubt that the United States was bent on the dismantlement of the British preferential system at the moment when Britain was at its weakest to resist any demands, it can be seen in Clause IV of the Atlantic Charter. Drawn up by President Roosevelt and Mr Churchill at sea off Newfoundland in August 1941, Clause IV spoke of "access on equal terms to the trade and raw materials of the world" : Churchill managed to repulse this particular attack on imperial preference by inserting a caveat, "with due respect to their existing obligations". The Secretary of State, Cordell Hull, was nothing if not consistent and in the course of seeking to prevent Japan's economic absorption of China confided to the Japanese Ambassador in October 1941 "that he had been fighting such measures as those taken at Ottawa and would like to have Japan join with the United States in fighting for liberal economic policies". The Japanese reply was to attack Pearl Harbor.

Drawn irretrievably into the war, the United States set about defining where her vital interest lay. In the preamble to the Mutual Aid (Lend Lease) Agreement the United States faced the fact that "the defence of the United Kingdom against aggression is vital to the defence of the United States". Nevertheless, although President Roosevelt was to claim that it "took the dollar sign" out of Anglo-American co-operation, Article VII of the Agreement included the aim of "the elimination of all forms of discriminatory treatment in international commerce, and . . . the reduction of tariffs and other trade barriers . . .". In private correspondence with President Roosevelt the British Prime

Minister secured assent to the proposition "that we were no more committed to the abolition of Imperial Preference than the American Government were committed to the abolition of their high protective tariffs" (Winston Churchill's speech to the House of Commons on 1 April 1944). In some senses Article VII of the Mutual Aid Agreement was a more important commitment, certainly in the eyes of the US State Department, than the corresponding passage in the Atlantic Charter if only because the United States had by then become a party to the war and need no longer be automatically conceded its demands. As the war progressed, however, the predominance of the American war machine and industrial back-up effort over that of the combined British Empire was to strengthen the American bargaining position. The corresponding decline in British strength as Britain mortgaged its future by selling off much of its worldwide foreign investments accentuated the disparity between the two major English-speaking allies.

The idea that at any point during World War II Britain was anything more than a junior partner in the alliance with the United States was always a fiction. It was a fiction made credible by the heroic stature of Winston Churchill's leadership and the united response of the British Empire at an earlier date than either of the two titans, the United States or the Soviet Union, were willing to make their stand against the Axis Powers. In the context of the events which we have just described this may seem an unnecessary point to make, but, in the light of the events of the postwar period and the subsequent attempts to claim that the "special relationship" was dead because of the diminution of British power, it reveals a fundamental misconception of the character of the "special relationship". Both during World War II and the Cold War which succeeded it the "special relationship" was as much an American device to secure the closest possible collaboration of its most consistently loyal ally as it was a means for Britain first of achieving victory and later of maintaining its territorial integrity. Sentiment there may have been, but beneath it lay the raw reality of national interest. That there were as many conflicting national interests as there were common objectives was one of those aspects of the relationship which those involved fully appreciated. Moreover, that the stronger of the two powers was likely to achieve its long-term objectives even at the expense of the weaker was never even momentarily questioned by its chief American practitioners.

The first intimation of this reality was to be seen in the ending of Lend Lease the moment hostilities ceased. The fact that Britain had geared her whole economy to winning the war meant that she was far from ready to sustain a peacetime role just like that. Not only had she sold foreign investments which halved her invisible income from abroad, but her whole economy, instead of being directed to exporting manufactures, had been switched to producing essential war materials. In the closing stages of the war around 68 per cent of Britain's productive capacity was devoted to the war effort in one way or another compared with only 12 per cent of America's total capacity, gigantic though it was by comparison. Instead of encouraging the strengthening of the Commonwealth preference system which had helped Britain to recover from the slump of the 1930s, or at least adopting a policy of non-intervention, the State Department, perceiving British weakness, was more than ever determined to erode the preference system and abolish sterling as a reserve currency. The fact that in 1938 something like 80 per cent of Britain's trade was carried out with the preference-area countries and that the same countries absorbed considerably in excess of half Britain's total exports, far from being seen as the most obvious means of resuscitating an exhausted and heavily indebted nation, was wilfully and singlemindedly disregarded by the now all-powerful State Department planners.

For the next thirty years the basic premises upon which US foreign economic policy rested included an almost unchallenged assumption that the British preference system should be ended. The irony was that by 1975 the Commonwealth system of preferences had been drastically run down, where they had not been terminated, only to be replaced by a European preferential system far more extensive and infinitely more discriminatory overall, despite the Lomé agreements, than the British one that it had supplanted. During these three decades three men, each in their separate ways men of quite outstanding distinction, were to dominate the formulation and execution of US foreign policy towards Britain : Dean Acheson, John Foster Dulles and George Ball. General George C. Marshall, who preceded Acheson as Secretary of State, may fairly be regarded as the great mobilizer of the US armed forces and as such one of the chief architects of the eventual Allied victory. His crowning achievement in the shape of the Marshall Plan, which was to successfully put the occupied countries of Western Europe on their feet by a rehabilitation programme combining emergency aid with self-help measures, was, however, only marginally concerned with Britain.

Acheson, Dulles and Ball shared the common characteristics of being lawyers, non-elected public servants and profoundly committed to checkmate the expansionist ambitions of the Soviet Union. All three, though their respective styles of diplomacy offer a study in contrasts, were effective exponents of the idealist as opposed to the realist approach to foreign affairs to which Dr Henry Kissinger belongs. As lawyers they had a powerful natural instinct, even flair, for fixing arrangements which were likely to serve the cause of America's immediate interests, often regarded as identical with that of each of the Western powers. Although this took on differing aspects, Acheson, Dulles and Ball all held steadfastly to the idea of the indispensability of legal arrangements, especially treaties, to confer legitimacy on whatever new arrangements they had jointly devised with their allies of the moment. As non-elected officials they had the great practical advantage that they could pursue their strategic objectives with a singlemindedness often denied the elected official— that is, as long as they retained the complete confidence of their democratically elected political masters. Acheson, Dulles and Ball were in fact notably successful in maintaining the confidence of Presidents Truman, Eisenhower and Kennedy respectively, and to a lesser extent President Johnson. Indeed, a strong case can be made for maintaining that, certainly in regard to Britain and Western Europe, they, rather than the President, decided the basic posture which America adopted during their years of office. They were successful and enthusiastic executors of presidential policies for the very reason that they had themselves fed their political masters with the essential policies for which the Presidents ultimately became responsible.

Their ideological presuppositions were dominated by a single overweening fact : the brute Soviet hegemony exercised over Eastern Europe and the declared expansionist aims of Stalin and his successors. In adoptng a mental attitude akin to a crusade to resist Soviet Communism each of these American statesmen perceived the Soviet empire as the central factor with which US foreign policy would have to contend for at least a generation. Since Soviet military power was most heavily concentrated in Europe, whence the Russian heartland had been ravaged by both Napoleon and Hitler, it was almost inevitable that the

United States should match Soviet hegemony with a hegemony of its own in Western Europe. It would be difficult to dispute that such a policy has effectively given Western Europe a span of thirty years to recover; moreover, that although the United States is the most powerful single military and economic power in Western Europe, as the Soviet Union is indubitably in Eastern Europe, there has been a general renaissance in national political and economic power, particularly in West Germany and France. In other words, the foreign policy pursued by the "European firsters" in the US State Department who must include both Acheson and Ball who were predominantly preoccupied with the resuscitation of Europe, and Dulles too, who regarded NATO as the linchpin of the entire arc of defence pacts which he laboriously constructed to contain the Soviet Union, must be regarded a resounding success in the achievement of its primary objective. That it contained significant flaws was only to be expected.

First, as lawyers, Acheson, Dulles and Ball were more interested in winning the immediate arguments than questioning whether their assumptions—about the means of building a permanent alliance community to resist the Soviet threat—were correct ones. Secondly, as non-elected officials, they had little or no feel for the democratic process in either the United States or Europe. Unsurprisingly they were not too choosy over whether the European comity they were to foster would be a democratic structure. Their concern was a simple one, that Western Europe should be strong and that it should speak as one. Third, in the pursuit of American national security, a legitimate interest inextricably bound up with Western Europe's own survival, America's chief foreign policy architects failed to see the irony that in the process of safeguarding America's national sovereignty they were urging the Europeans to surrender theirs in a federal system of some sort. It is not hard to see how citizens of a democratic federation, which on the whole had succeeded, should assume its virtues appropriate for the semi-continent of Western Europe, hitherto divided since the days of the Roman Empire, except for brief periods under dictators such as Charlemagne, Napoleon and Hitler. Equally understandable is the fact that a nation, a former great power, whose independent history extends unbroken for a thousand years should hesitate to pool its sovereignty in a federation of unspecified character. That, in the jargon of the diplomatic trade, the United States as a great power, indeed as one of two global super-powers, had the right, even the obligation, to influence what is called "the milieu" of Western Europe need not be seriously questioned. That these ambitions to reshape "the milieu" were often based on highly unreal assumptions in the form of idealist illusions can be judged by the events about to be described.

If one man can be said to represent the fountain-head of the idealist school which dominated American foreign policy in the middle years of the twentieth century that man must be President Woodrow Wilson. In his lofty aspirations and valiant efforts in pursuit of the establishment of a new world order, his belief in the inevitability and perfectability of human progress, and in the creative role that America could play in fashioning the new world order, Wilson profoundly affected both Acheson and Dulles. He was in truth the very counterpoint of his revolutionary contemporary, Lenin, as Dulles was to tacitly acknowledge in distributing copies of Lenin's plans for world conquest while he indefatigably rallied the countries of the free world which Wilson had championed forty years before. But first to Acheson.

Dean Acheson had been a Washington lawyer for around ten years when President Franklin Roosevelt appointed him Under Secretary of the Treasury in May 1933. He resigned only six months later over Roosevelt's gold purchase plan and might have never reappeared but for World War II, when he became Assistant Secretary of State in 1941 and Under Secretary of State in 1945 where he remained until June 1947. This was a crucial formative period in Anglo-American relations if only because Britain was so weak and America so obviously dominant. It was on the face of it a period of extraordinary creativity not to say magnanimity in American foreign policy towards Europe.

Nevertheless there were aspects of both the Bretton Woods monetary system, which helped shape the economic character of the postwar world for a generation, and even the Marshall Plan, which raised Europe to its feet, that represented a clear-cut assertion of American interests, simultaneously aimed at cutting the British system down to size. In Article VIII of the International Monetary Fund's charter drawn up at Bretton Woods there is a section forbidding members to engage in or allow any discriminatory currency arrangements or multiple currency practices except as authorized by the agreement or subsequently by the Fund. This was expressly designed to undercut the sterling system and to maintain an exchange system fixed to gold, or in practical terms the dollar, since America held more than 80 per cent of the world's monetary gold. Moreover, even the Marshall Plan, which stands as an historic milestone in the history of relations between states in the twentieth century in the scope of its generosity, contained the familiar incentives to create a customs union for Western Europe, pointedly disregarding the fact that such a solution would run counter to the Commonwealth system which still accounted for three-quarters of Britain's trade. The paramount American interests were clear enough and were succinctly expressed in the Harriman Report (itself an assessment of the proposals of the Paris Committee of the Marshall Plan), which stressed the great strategic and political as well as economic interests that America had at stake in postwar Western Europe.

Although Acheson had left government in June 1947, the same month that General Marshall unveiled his plan for reviving Western Europe in a celebrated speech he gave at Harvard, he had been intimately involved for the previous six years in the formulation of America's various plans and programmes to re-create the postwar world but especially the major battleground of Western Europe. The establishment of UNRRA, the calling of the Bretton Woods Conference and the Marshall Plan were all of a piece. America being the most powerful of the Western powers, Acheson saw a legitimate underlying pursuit of American foreign policy as the shaping of conditions abroad "so as to maintain an environment favourable to our interests".[1]

Thus when in January 1949 he returned to government after an eighteen-month absence, this time as General Marshall's successor as Secretary of State, Acheson wasted no time in assessing his priorities. He had known them for a long time. He pressed ahead during 1949 and 1950 with the creation of the North Atlantic Treaty Organization, which must be rated his most signal single achievement and which was to provide the indispensable military framework behind which both Europe and America have sheltered ever since. His desire to create a European Defence Community was less auspicious and left to

[1] Dean Acheson, *A Democrat Looks at His Party*, Harper, New York, 1955. See also Paul Nitz, Annex A, The Purpose of United States Military and Economic Assistance from the study submitted to the President's Committee to Study the US Military Assistance Programme, March, 1959.

the next Secretary of State, Dulles, a legacy which he was unable to exploit. In the Far East, in the implementation of Truman's decision to intervene in Korea and in his judicious appointment of Dulles to draw up and negotiate the Japanese Peace Treaty, he demonstrated his diplomatic acumen, skills of which President Kennedy was later to avail himself following the disaster of the Bay of Pigs. In the four years of Acheson's Secretaryship he was deeply preoccupied with holding the ring against an expansionist Soviet Union, a task in which he was generally judged to have been successful. It was during his period as a senior foreign policy adviser to Kennedy a decade later that his penchant for seeing foreign policy in pre-eminently military terms may have made Kennedy himself make the military objectives of US foreign policy in Europe his almost exclusive and certainly his foremost concern. Meanwhile the conduct of US foreign policy in the intervening decade was to be dominated by one of the most controversial of all US Secretaries of State.

John Foster Dulles, the most redoubtable Western protagonist of the Cold War, was born to the Secretaryship even if he had not set his sights upon it at a very early age. His maternal grandfather, John Watson Foster, was Secretary of State under President Benjamin Harrison while by the time Dulles was in his late twenties Robert Lansing, his uncle by marriage, was appointed Secretary of State in the cabinet of President Wilson. A child of the manse, Dulles attended Princeton and George Washington Universities and finally the Sorbonne before joining a leading New York law firm as a specialist in international law in 1911. His first opportunity to demonstrate his skills at the highest level arose when at the age of thirty he was named by President Wilson as legal counsel to the US delegation to the Versailles Peace Conference. Like the young Franklin Roosevelt, Wilson's Secretary for the Navy, Dulles absorbed something of the President's idealism for the construction of a new world order and a belief that this new order could be hastened into being by treaties. A quarter of a century later Dulles helped draw up the UN Charter at Dumbarton Oaks and acted as legal counsel to the inaugural conference of the UN at San Francisco. He was thus a fairly obvious choice for Acheson when the terms of a Japanese Peace Treaty came to be negotiated. The Treaty, signed in 1951, may yet prove the most enduring and creative reminder of his particular brand of diplomatic and legal skills.

When he became President Dwight D. Eisenhower's Secretary

of State in January 1953 Dulles was already sixty-five. For the next six years, with Eisenhower's full-hearted support, Dulles with indefatigable determination set about extending the anti-Communist alliance system which had been begun in Europe. From the south-eastern flank of NATO grew an interlocking alliance system composed of the Central Treaty Organization and the South-East Asia Treaty Organization powers which ranged all the pro-US Asian states in an anti-Communist latter-day Great Wall of South Asia. If NATO was to prove a good investment the new alliances were to prove something of an embarrassment, more of a provocation to internal insurrection than an effective guarantee against Soviet and Chinese aggression. In the sense that they presupposed that the peoples of Asia were as anxious to preserve the status quo as those of Western Europe (an unjustified presupposition) the alliance system and the mental approach which accompanied it led inexorably to the nightmare of Vietnam. Much of this is now widely accepted. Yet the assumptions which underlay US policy in Asia then differ little from the assumption which continues to underlie US policy in Europe now. Namely, that the overriding requirement of the United States is that Europe remains anti-Soviet in its basic alignment. As President Gerald Ford's Secretary of Defense James Schlesinger put it recently, the object of US foreign policy, not least in Europe, is "to maintain freedom abroad". The assumption then, as now, was that freedom could be equated with an anti-Communist regime or, more specifically still, an anti-Soviet regime. Hence the United States has made alliances with many nations which in the past have been far from democratic—in Europe, Portugal, Spain, Greece and Turkey for example. The use of the phrase "freedom abroad" grew from Woodrow Wilson's concept of the right of national self-determination to the Dullesian policy of maintaining "freedom abroad" in the sense that the alliances constructed were designed to thwart the absorption of the nations concerned into the Soviet imperium. Given the nature of the ties between the Soviet Union and its satellites, this was a legitimate use of the word freedom. Its obvious weakness lay in its implicit and narrowly ideological definition of the word freedom, as if autocracy was a monopoly of the Left and of the Soviet Union. The truth is that the objective of "freedom abroad", consistently pursued by the United States since the days of Dulles, is not designed to take account of political freedom in the internal sense but only in terms of freedom from an external threat, e.g. the Soviet Union. This is important to remember when we examine the promotion of West European unity by the United States and the absence of strong democratic structures in the central machinery, or the major continental component states, of the enlarged EEC of the 1970s. Moreover, America's attitudes towards Europe have differed from those towards other continents and countries primarily in the level of US involvement rather than in the nature of her objectives.

That Dulles saw American foreign policy objectives as being essentially the same in Europe as they were in Asia and that therefore the means employed should be broadly the same is generally acknowledged. Rarely in history have great powers been called upon to evolve what are effectively global foreign policies. It is not therefore surprising that in seeking to apply a coherent grand design, whatever plan was devised would prove inadequate to deal with the complexities that inevitably arose.

At the end of a worldwide conflict the United States emerged as one of the two most powerful victors. Since the other major victor was committed to a programme of world conquest and on recent evidence had every intention of fulfilling that ambition, the United States accepted the role of a global power almost without realizing the immensity of the task history had thrust upon her. Into this global framework a man like Dulles fitted perfectly. The trouble is that the framework was more apparent than real. Not only did the Communist world not constitute a monolithic whole, but the non-Communist world was even more fissiparous and even less susceptible to being dragooned into service against the Communists.

To illustrate: when Dulles, as part of his grand defensive design, insisted on the formation of the European Defence Community in 1953 (which, as we saw in the chapter on the Labour Party, held frightening potential for any would-be dictator), he threatened to polarize the entire free world. As he himself put it in a phrase that has since entered the language, failure by France to ratify the EDC would result in an "agonizing reappraisal" of US relations with France, and, by inference, with Western Europe as a whole. Having been three times invaded by Germanic forces within the space of seventy years the French could hardly be blamed for being chary about entrusting their security to a military organization, as yet unproven in peace let alone war, which gave enormous powers to the German military commanders. The primacy, in American eyes, of the military factor in the reconstitution of Europe could not be more plainly shown, nor the supreme American indifference to the absence of democratic checks on an unprecedented concentration of European military power. Like the corporation lawyer that he had been for so long, Dulles was bent on achieving success for his client, in this case the United States. From such a style brinkmanship inevitably resulted, brinkmanship practised without discrimination on friend and foe alike.

Dulles had three prevailing passions in his conduct of foreign policy. They were his fanatical anti-Communism, his belief in the efficacy of treaties, and, not least, his belief in himself and the rightness of his cause. At no time were these three abiding passions brought together so dramatically as in the events leading up to the Anglo-French debacle at Suez in 1956. In a word, Suez was the epitome of Dullesian brinkmanship. There is no reason to doubt that Dulles was sincere when he said he believed that, once Nasser had bought arms from the Soviet Union, Egypt would turn against the United States. Hence Dulles' decision in July 1956 to turn down Nasser's request for aid to build the Aswan Dam. If Dulles had held a more sophisticated view of international relations he would have perceived that the Aswan Dam, symbol of the new Egypt, was worth a great deal more to the United States in diplomatic terms than any arms Egypt might buy from the Soviet Union. His decision, which virtually pulled the rug of Egypt's future prosperity and her aspirations to become a modern state from under Nasser's feet, was to lead effectively to a power vacuum which the Soviet Union quickly filled and occupied unchallenged from 1958 until 1973. If Dulles' most significant overall achievement was to keep Soviet expansion within bounds during the 1950s, his policies in the Middle East were to have the very reverse effect.

Since Suez Britain has not undertaken any major foreign policy initiative without first securing American political, military and financial support. It is also true that to some extent, even among those who opposed the Anglo-French intervention, Suez was to many Britons a "let-down" experience in Anglo-American relations such as Vietnam was also to represent to many Americans a decade later. The significance of Suez to the theme of this chapter is that it illustrated both the preponderance of US power and the determination of the United States to use that preponderance to the very utmost. Even a modicum of candour by Dulles towards Britain and France before the event could have forestalled its pathetic fulfilment. Since Krushchev's threat to bomb London and Paris was incapable of fulfilment, it was the United States which effectively crushed its chief European allies. Suez also sounded the death knell of Britain's far flung imperial legacy, incidentally turning the temperamental imperialists in the Conservative Party and the Foreign Office towards Europe. Those who accepted the validity of a Commonwealth based on mutual economic and political interests, with no fundamental necessity for Britain to dominate such an association, were to be far less depressed by Suez, constitutional and military questions aside. For them the Empire and its inevitable military hangover was now dead; long live the Commonwealth.

Nasser, publicly spurned by the United States, had nationalized and proceeded to occupy the Suez Canal. Dulles responded by calling Nasser "nothing but a tin-horn Hitler". The words were to provide what proved to be a fatal form of encouragement to the British Prime Minister, Anthony Eden, who after all had played an heroic role in personally standing up to both Hitler and Stalin in the 1930s and 1940s. The ill-conceived Anglo-French military intervention, under pretext of separating the Israeli and Egyptian forces, is now history. There are many unanswered questions, but the paramount one which should concern us is: did Dulles realize the full nature of the provocation he was offering? He probably did not fully appreciate the seriousness of Nasser's loss of face, but then he also had written Nasser off as far as US influence was concerned. Dulles believed emphatically that neither Britain nor France had any place in the Middle East whatsoever, but did he appreciate the degree of Britain's economic dependence on her Commonwealth partners, for which the Canal was an apparently indispensable link? The answer is that he probably understood this very well. When the Anglo-French invasion took place he was not personally too shocked; he detested Nasser and he believed that treaties were inviolate, but he also saw the opportunity to demonstrate to the entire world Britain's economic and ultimately military weakness and utter dependence on the United States. The lesson was well learnt.

Following World War II, with the considerable impetus of

nationalist movements which had gained strength during the war, and the blessing of the postwar Attlee Government and all subsequent administrations, the Empire was gradually run down and transformed into a Commonwealth. This particular transformation, because it was historically unique and had only very approximate and much more limited parallels in the run down of the French and Dutch empires, was never remotely comprehended by the US State Department. The US policies, especially the foreign economic policies, which had been evolved to combat the British Empire with a moral fervour which only a former colony could have bred, were maintained against the Commonwealth with unabated determination. The change from Empire to Commonwealth, virtually disregarded by the State Department, involved many important aspects of the relationships between its members, not least the sovereign nature of each national government. The Empire was in some senses rather like a commercial company with a chairman (the sovereign) and a managing director (the British Prime Minister). By contrast, the Commonwealth was much more akin to a club where each member has equal rights, where seniority is respected but where innovations by new members are welcomed. At the core of the Empire was an administrative framework which placed Britain at the hub of a political and commercial system supported by seapower and the occasional garrison. By 1914 that Empire had visibly begun to set. Ironically, while backing the anti-colonialist movements (which were effectively anti-European) from 1917, both America and Russia steadily assumed imperialist roles, as we have already noted. The Chinese, seeing this, coined a new word for the latter day imperialist non-imperialists: the hegemonists.

The fall of Singapore mid-way through World War II represented the beginning of the end of the British Empire in Asia. From that date Australia and New Zealand joined Canada in realizing that their military guarantor from now on was to be the United States. The United States, in perceiving this change, tended to underestimate the strength of the political and economic, not to mention the cultural and familial ties which remained, especially with Australia and New Zealand, and even South Africa. By contrast with the Empire's indispensable backing of military capability which had clearly been fading since World War I, the Commonwealth's essential characteristic was that of a loose political association but one which had a very concrete series of bilateral and increasingly multilateral economic ties with no more than a string of token military bases to hold the ring. Such was America's preoccupation with the military aspect that she underestimated the economic and cultural (i.e. governmental and legal) legacy that not only survived but flourished. In the reality of this legacy lies some of the supra-military reasons why Britain was able to conduct successful counter-insurgency operations in Malaya and Borneo and de-escalate the confrontation between Malaysia and Indonesia, whereas America fought an infinitely costly war in Vietnam to an indefinite conclusion. The difference was that Britain precisely because she was only a middle-sized power, manifestly intent on withdrawing, could play the role of a policeman with some credibility. From her long experience she also understood what was required, particularly what was required in meeting the insurgents' demands in political and social terms. By contrast the United States introduced its pacification programme late in the day, as somewhat of an afterthought. Beneath the no doubt sincerely held claims that America's aim was to safeguard democracy, to thwart the fulfilment of the domino theory in south-east Asia, there was always the unmistakable glint of steel glimpsed through the imperial purple toga.

Against this background the crusade of the US State Department—epitomized in the West Point speech of Dean Acheson already quoted—assumes grandly ironic proportions. It was the very fact that the Commonwealth had, as Acheson put it, "no political structure, or unity or strength and enjoys a fragile and precarious economic relationship by means of the sterling area and preferences in the British market" that had meant it deserved and was able to survive until now. Unlike the growing Soviet and American imperia it was a threat to nobody yet conferred benefits on all its members, all of whom were free to leave at any time. Moreover, more effectively than any other grouping it maintained contact between the industrialized and non-industrialized nations, with much the most generous trading arrangements in the form of access for agricultural exports to the markets of the industrialized partners. All of this was seen with great clarity by none other than President Charles de Gaulle, who recognized in the Commonwealth the enormous past and potential source of Britain's strength. The development of the French Union during his Presidency shows signs that he valued the Commonwealth as an example of inter-continental, north-south partnership, although he obviously had infinitely less to work with and a very different colonial legacy. His cultivation of France's relations with Quebec, Tahiti and even remotest New Caledonia is perhaps a clue to the kind of attention he might have bestowed on Canada, Australia and New Zealand had he, rather than a succession of British Prime Ministers (who after Eden took them very much for granted for the most part), inherited the leadership of the British Commonwealth. It is inconceivable that had France, under almost any leader, been allied to Canada, Australia and New Zealand with political, economic and cultural ties comparable with those that Britain possessed, she would have treated this source of strength with such scant respect. Not only were the economies of Britain and the Old Dominions of a complementary character, which was hardly an accident, but the fund of goodwill and built-in advantages enjoyed by Britain at governmental, company and individual level was incalculable. In the light of the ties which the United States and Japan have subsequently established with each of these three countries it is nothing short of incredible that Britain did not perceive the value of giving the highest priority to these links. Britain's displacement by the United States and Japan, while it is a fact, was in no sense automatic but rather stemmed from a confusion of Britain's priorities and a false appreciation of where Britain's long-term interests lay.

It is idle to speculate why the US State Department, from such an early period, felt the necessity to attack the Commonwealth as it had the Empire before it. There was no comparison between the two. Moreover the Commonwealth, as Acheson's remarks make clear, was in no sense a rival to the United States in either the political or economic sense. Did the United States understand for instance why Canada, whose economy was clearly bound to that of her own, remained a member of the Commonwealth? The reasons may have been uncomfortable ones for the United States to face but they were inescapable. Canada's membership of the Commonwealth was a means of maintaining her identity separate from that of the United States. It was also a unique forum in which Canada could play a constructive role of her own in the international arena. The evidence suggests that the US State Department understood this very well indeed but felt it would be more convenient if Canada, like the Latin American states, could be allied economically almost exclusively to the United States. One cannot escape the suspicion that behind the anti-Commonwealth bias of the United States there was the ill-concealed desire of the United States to displace British influence in political no less than economic terms. It may indeed demonstrate a principle, namely that it takes an emergent imperialist power to effectively denude a former colonial empire of its economic life-blood as distinct from its political structure (which was shed relatively painlessly). The fact that Britain needed a worldwide set of special economic relationships merely to sustain her role as a medium-sized industrial nation, without any pretensions to great-power status, was quite lost on the State Department as the policies they were to promote unmistakably reveal.

It is not without irony that the great European bogeyman of the British Europeanists in the 1960s, President Charles de Gaulle, understood the reality of Britain's political and economic situation with supreme clarity, certainly with greater clarity than America's foreign policy planners and possibly more clearly than many of Britain's own political leaders. De Gaulle vetoed British entry twice for three quite concrete and comprehensible reasons. First, he wanted France's position of dominance within the Community to be consolidated against the day when German economic strength would be expressed in political terms. The longer Britain could be kept out, and he foresaw Britain as a more natural ally of Germany than France on the majority of questions, the more readily could France shape the Community and perpetuate her national advantages. Second, and following on the logic of the first point, de Gaulle saw the Commonwealth as an integral element of Britain's whole economic structure and international competitiveness. Britain could only enter in his Presidency if she were prepared to strip herself of all those vital connections which had contributed so materially to her strength in the past. As de Gaulle foresaw with some presience, only Edward Heath among Britain's leading politicians was prepared to pay such a price. Third, de Gaulle saw British entry as a Trojan horse for the United States. Already the United States was the most powerful military and economic power in Western Europe. With Britain within the Community, especially if Britain were to be relatively strong, de Gaulle feared she would become the political lever for US interests. Naturally the United States denied vehemently that this was ever their intention and the British certainly did not see themselves as a Trojan horse for anyone. Nevertheless, as the succeeding pages demonstrate, this was a generally fair assessment of American intentions.

But why did the United States wish to employ Britain as a Trojan horse? Was it in Woodrow Wilson's oft-repeated phrase to "make the world safe for democracy" by providing a political grouping in Western Europe that would make political decision-taking in defence as in other matters that much more predictable, more orientated towards the defence of the West as a whole? No doubt this was a major consideration. At the same time the United States, as a super-power whose position rested on its military and economic strength, had never been averse to restricting the role of the British in the economic sphere, as we have already seen, more especially if it impinged on the rate of American economic expansion. To the extent that trade and investment tend to go together, the Commonwealth had always represented a slight rein on US economic influence. Now that Britain was obviously no longer able to play the part of a world economic power nothing seemed more logical than that she should join the new European Economic Community, providing in the process a bridgehead for American political and economic influence in Western Europe. Britain, so the argument ran, as America's most loyal ally, could be relied upon to appreciate the American position even if it would not always risk pleading the American case. Despite the obvious fallacy of this particular line of argument—namely that Britain stripped of her worldwide connections would merely revert to what she had been before she acquired a worldwide commercial empire, an offshore island of Europe, a weakling economically, politically and diplomatically—all this was swept aside in the interests of pursuing the neater, more logical, solution of tying Britain irrevocably to Europe as a form of insurance against the development of a vaguely anti-American, possibly slightly neutralist Western Europe. To understand why the United States adopted this policy of promoting British entry into the EEC in the first instance and subsequently pursued it with very little wavering throughout the Kennedy, Johnson and Nixon administrations we must examine the career of the third major architect of US foreign policy towards Europe in the postwar period.

Unlike both Acheson and Dulles, who achieved worldwide recognition as justly celebrated Secretaries of State, George Ball never attained the post of Secretary, which was held during his period as Under Secretary by Dean Rusk. The important fact about Ball, however, was that he had the full confidence of the President, which meant ready access to him; in the end, there is not much doubt that he rather than Kennedy himself was drawing up and executing US policy towards Europe, certainly in its most formative early stages. These are large claims but they are sustainable even on the admittedly incomplete evidence so far available. But was George Ball, like Acheson and Dulles, born to the purple too? He was not. Born in the mid-West, in Des Moines, Iowa in 1909, Ball was educated at Northwestern University law school near Chicago where he graduated in 1933, the year in which Roosevelt appointed Acheson Under Secretary to the Treasury. It was of course another mid-Western lawyer, a Chicagoan, Adlai Stevenson, descended from a former Vice-President, who from being Governor of Illinois became the Democratic presidential candidate in 1952 and 1956 and, as titular head of the Democratic Party for most of the 1950s, devoted himself to formulating a global foreign policy for the United States. He was an obvious candidate to become Kennedy's Secretary of State but since Kennedy wished to direct foreign policy personally he chose an administrator of great skill in Dean Rusk to head the State Department. Had Stevenson been appointed Secretary of State the career of George Ball, the international fixer, would have been severely circumscribed. The European policies of the United States, and especially the promotion of British entry into the EEC, might have been pursued with greater attention to the other options available. For Stevenson, twice defeated presidential candidate, had seized his unique position to make a succession of world tours to familiarize himself with the true situation abroad, thereby making himself the best informed prospective Secretary of State in US history. His non-appointment to the top foreign policy job was to prove a costly error for the Kennedy Administration and the American people resulting in fundamentally misconceived American policies towards both Vietnam and Western Europe.

George Ball began his legal career in government service in Washington. After an interim period practising law in Chicago he returned to Washington in 1942 to become associate general counsel for the Lend Lease Administration and later director of the US Strategic Bombing Survey in London. He had by now firmly established himself as a European specialist with top-level connections. Thus when he quit government service in 1946 to found his own law firm it was only natural that he should not only specialize in international law but in European affairs. Before long the founders of the EEC and its embryo organizations were among his clients; later he played a direct role as a legal adviser to the West European unification movement. This experience as an insider in the creation of the new framework for Western Europe, devised exclusively by continental Europeans, was to prove invaluable when he came to deal with the same people as the official representative of the US Government. Equally, the founders of the EEC found it an immeasurable advantage to have one of their own, so to speak, at the elbow of the President, totally committed to their vision of the new Europe and willing to employ every means available to harmonize American and Europeanist (effectively Franco-German) interests.

Even before John Kennedy had been inaugurated, Ball was appointed by the President-elect to head a task force to draw up a comprehensive programme of trade and tariff reform proposals. The tariff-cutting proposals which Ball came up with were subsequently incorporated into the Administration's programme and were to emerge eventually as the initiative which triggered the successful Kennedy Round of tariff reforms, more or less concluded in 1967. The general conception of these proposals was an admirable step in the direction of greater trade liberalization achieved by mutual multilateral concessions. It represented, together with the Test Ban Treaty, one of the most significant achievements of the Kennedy Administration in foreign policy. It contained, as we will see later, a skilfully contrived basket of measures which enabled British entry to be seen as part of a general set of proposals to liberalize world trade. The reality was something entirely different.

By this time Ball had become Under Secretary for Economic Affairs in the State Department, and by November 1961 he had become the principal Under Secretary for policy planning—the kind of role which Dulles would have retained for himself. In a real sense Ball was able to determine US foreign policy towards Europe, including Britain, for the next six years. In terms of British entry these years were critical not because they achieved the desired objective in the time expected—they did not—but because they established a consistent American commitment to British entry backed up by considerable sanctions. None of this is to imply that Kennedy did not himself have firm ideas of his own concerning Europe and the Anglo-American relationship, independently arrived at and owing nothing to George Ball.

What the evidence does suggest is that Ball's consistency of commitment, his understanding of the chief factors at work including the people who could carry policy measures, and above all the points where leverage could be applied, were unerring and practically indispensable to the carrying out of Kennedy's and Johnson's policies towards Europe and British membership of the EEC. At no time is the awesome power which Ball so discreetly wielded better illustrated than in the meeting which took place between him and Edward Heath on 30 March 1961.

At the time of course Heath had been entrusted by Macmillan with Britain's entry negotiations. Ball knew that Heath, more than any other British politician, was determined on British entry. His commitment, for instance, was far greater than that of Macmillan who was inhibited by Britain's ties with the Commonwealth which he sincerely valued though underestimating their importance. For Heath, as for Ball, British entry was an *idée fixe* to which all else was subordinated. Such was Ball's confidence in his ability to carry the young President that he freely admits that when he met Heath on this occasion he had not previously discussed with Kennedy the specific question which Heath put to him, namely the extent of American backing of British entry. This in no way inhibited him, Ball, from giving the most forthright and expansive of replies in the following terms.

> If Britain is now prepared to recognise that the Rome Treaty is not a static document but a process that could eventually lead to an evolving European Community—something in the nature of a European federation—and if Britain can make the great national decision to join Europe on these terms, I am confident that my government will regard this as a major contribution to Western solidarity and the stability of the free world. So long as Britain remains outside the European Community she is a force for division rather than cohesion, since she is like a giant lodestar drawing with unequal degrees of force on each member state. But if Great Britain now decides to participate in the formidable efforts to unite Europe she can and I am sure will apply her unique political genius— in which we have great confidence—towards the creation of a unity that can transform the Western world. (George Ball, *The Discipline of Power*, The Bodley Head, p. 79.)

Here we have a clear and concise declaration of the official

American vision of Britain's future in Europe. Ball argues that a federation, a unified Western Europe of some sort is a necessary ingredient to the "creation of a unity that can transform the Western world". There is a touching naivety—or is it merely flattery—in the expression of faith in Britain's "unique political genius" as if it were something every Briton carried in his knapsack, rather than something evolved and fought for down the centuries and safeguarded in institutions and constitutional precedents which, as a result of entry, were to be directly supplanted. Above all else Ball's goal is unity, and the form that takes and the means to its achievement are assumed to be matters of merely tactical importance. It was a general attitude that Edward Heath shared, though his intention was that Britain might find the means significantly to shape the new Europe.

Thus when Ball left his meeting with Heath he felt in a confident mood. At last the British Government seemed willing to accept the idea of both a common external tariff system (somewhat at odds with previous US policy let alone Britain's own history, one is bound to note) and the Community's principal political institutions, the Council of Ministers and the Commission. As Ball observed, he left the meeting with Heath "with a sense that something historic might have happened". In the sense that he had spoken to the man who had made an irrevocable commitment and was determined to carry it through, at any price, his sense of the historicity of the occasion was almost certainly justified. Ball's confidence was not entirely shared by his colleagues in the State Department, nor in the US Cabinet, which still held to the position, evolved since the days of the Marshall Plan, that a merger between the Six (the EEC) and the Seven (EFTA), uniting the greater part of Western Europe, was the more important objective. Had the United States given such a goal priority over promoting British entry into the EEC the chances are that a wider but much looser form of unity might have been achieved relatively painlessly, something along the lines of an expanded free trade area for all of Western Europe which might later have embraced the North American NATO partners at an appropriate moment. But having worked for and within the EEC movement Ball was ideologically and emotionally totally committed to the EEC alternative, which in terms of its strategic development as a political partner and military ally of the United States would only be effective if

Britain joined its ranks. Ball's experience with Lend Lease, with the Strategic Bombing Survey had left him with an awareness of the advantages of a strong central political structure if the threat from the East was to be successfully outfaced. Kennedy adopted the Ball stance not only because it appealed to his desire to foster a visibly strong political framework but also because he sensed that he had the man to carry it through to its completion. He was almost right.

Thus when Macmillan came to Washington to see Kennedy in April 1961 the ground had been well prepared on the precise European alternative that America favoured, Kennedy enthusiastically endorsing Ball's position. The whole atmosphere which Ball had helped to create engendered confidence in a British entry bid, which it was assumed was bound to succeed, not least because it had the backing of the United States. Macmillan's visit to Washington visibly strengthened his resolve to sign the Rome Treaty, which as Ball accurately explained was not an absolutist document but more of a framework upon which a pragmatic nation like Britain could build. The fascinating thing is that despite the tragic death of Kennedy by assassination, and the departure of Macmillan from Number 10 Downing Street, and not least the total rejection of Britain by de Gaulle in its first entry bid, Ball was to play exactly the same role in 1966 when Prime Minister Harold Wilson visited President Lyndon Johnson with precisely the same conclusion ahead, namely a French veto. Meanwhile in 1961 Ball recalls Macmillan saying that: "We are going to need some help from you in getting in—but we are going in. Yesterday was one of the greatest days of my life." Of the fact that this Washington meeting offered Macmillan renewed hope in the fulfilment of a long cherished personal ambition to have Britain join a European political union there can be no doubt.

Despite his excellent relations with his wartime superior and companion in arms, President Dwight D. Eisenhower, Macmillan realized that the Eisenhower Administration was not anxious to act hastily and encourage the too rapid development and expansion (which British entry might accentuate) of a West European union which showed signs of discriminating against US exports. He soon realized that under Ball's orchestration the Kennedy Administration was prepared to subordinate any economic problems for the United States to the achievement of a political goal of European union, considered of vast importance to America and the free world.

Reading the American purpose as he did, Macmillan, who set great practical and sentimental value on the Anglo-American relationship, saw the significant modification in American goals and means at the policy-making level of US Government as an opportunity of forging even closer links with the Americans. On any evaluation this was a short-term view. As any diplomatist knows, major policy goals cannot be based on the personal compatibility of the current heads of government however much this may expedite immediate business. Should British entry into the EEC be successfully accomplished it was always much more likely to widen the differences between Britain and the United States if only because the new West European union would have far greater scope for conflict with the United States by virtue of its size and the wider range of competing interests that clearly existed in trade, monetary and defence matters.

Besides such perennial high policy questions there were more mundane issues which must have affected the Macmillan-Kennedy relationship and through them the whole spectrum of Anglo-American relations. Not least among them was the fact that Britain was seeking a loan of £714m from the United States and the International Monetary Fund. It was in truth difficult for Britain to pursue any other policy than that which the United States willed at any time in the postwar period, chiefly because of British weakness, but during the not infrequent periods when Britain was begging for US loans the possibility of British and US foreign policy seriously diverging became minimal. All this suited the Kennedy-Ball ground-plan perfectly. Since the British had very little room for manoeuvre the United States planners envisaged, though they could hardly state it in public, that Britain would be able to act as a counterweight to both France and Germany in the historic struggle for supremacy between them. By such means, that is by creating a greater equality among the three major component states of the Community, Kennedy hoped to pave the way for a political federation of Western Europe which would act as a theoretically equal but in practical terms less powerful partner to the United States. The new Community would inevitably be less powerful in political, economic and military terms because it would be a less mature entity and economic whole. By the time the Community had reached parity with the United States, assuming it ever did, the Soviet threat, Kennedy reasoned, would have either receded or disappeared.

In pursuance of these aims Kennedy left no stone unturned. In 1962 for instance, sensing he might be dealing with the next Labour Prime Minister, Kennedy assembled half his Cabinet in a vain attempt to convince the Labour Party leader, Hugh Gaitskell, that Britain's future lay in joining the EEC. Gaitskell remained unmoved and for reasons remarkably similar to President de Gaulle's reasons for keeping Britain out—namely that Britain's political and economic history was totally different from that of continental Europe; moreover, that it would be difficult if not impossible to unite the two without Britain, as the suppliant for entry, casting aside those aspects such as Parliament's supremacy, the Commonwealth economic system, etc., which Britain had evolved to suit her own particular requirements over a period of very nearly one thousand years. But if the concrete arguments lay with Gaitskell, the power lay with the Americans. And they did not hesitate to use it.

If any single piece of legislation epitomized the kind of authority wielded by George Ball in the campaign to propel Britain into the Community it was the US Trade Expansion Act. Designed to launch a multilateral series of tariff reductions, later known as the Kennedy Round, within the forum of the General Agreement on Tariffs and Trade, the Trade Expansion Act anticipated by a decade the US Trade Reform Act which launched the Nixon Round of trade reforms. The Trade Expansion Act was drawn up "as if Britain had joined the EEC", in other words the concessions that the United States was prepared to make were only available if Britain joined the Community. This move shrewdly applied pressure not only on Britain, and not only even on the original Six members of the EEC, but on all parties to the GATT negotiations. When Senators Henry Reuss of Wisconsin and Paul Douglas of Illinois put forward an amendment that would have allowed the implementation of the Act with or without British entry the Administration ruthlessly repressed it, though it would have in fact allowed a much greater measure of trade liberalization than the Act which was eventually passed by Congress. As Senator Reuss remarked: "The Trade Expansion Act was tailored to force Britain into the EEC."

Faced with the determined opposition of President de Gaulle even Ball's herculean efforts to engineer British entry came to naught. Ball's verdict on the first British entry attempt was that "It was a gallant and indefatigable effort but inevitably marred in technicalities. During the ensuing debate the British purpose became obscure, the political momentum was lost in niggardly bargaining." If entry at almost any political and economic price for Britain was the sole objective, as it was for Ball and as it became for Heath in the third and successful set of negotiations, this was a fair assessment. But if the vast differences in economic history and political procedures were squarely faced bargaining was a most necessary aspect of British entry. With no history of separate development to speak of compared with Europe, the founding fathers of the American confederation found protracted tariff negotiations an essential prerequisite for an enduring union.

Thus when the first negotiations opened in the autumn of 1961 it took eight months of preliminary fencing before the actual terms of a British accession became apparent. By putting on one side the most difficult questions such as agriculture and the length of the transitional period the negotiations made rapid progress in the succeeding four months, but the difficulties of reconciling Britain's system of cheap food and raw materials with a high-cost and highly protected European system remained. Kennedy, with Ball's encouragement, took the view that these problems could only be solved successfully from within the Community. His whole attitude was to view both the Commonwealth and EFTA as hostages of Britain's own making. It was a fundamental misappreciation on Kennedy's part. The Commonwealth and EFTA, as De Gaulle fully appreciated, were prime sources of British strength. Only a self-sufficient super-power like the United States could have failed to realize the degree to which Britain was dependent on her connections outside the EEC.

The negotiations of 1961–2 had no chance of succeeding, at any time, since unlike those of 1970, when only the terms of the transitional period were under negotiation, they were about the task of reconciling two entirely different systems. Whether Kennedy was right in believing that negotiations, i.e. true negotiations, could never succeed *except* from within the Community was put to the test when the Labour Government sought a renegotiation in the 1974–5 period. What is already known is that Kennedy resolutely opposed the maintenance of the Commonwealth preference arrangements except for the very shortest transitional period. This was at a time when British entry was being promoted in Britain as a means of expanding British export markets.

The view that Kennedy's personal interest in promoting Britain's entry into the EEC was almost exclusively for politico-strategic reasons is reinforced by his forceful opposition to the applications for associate membership of three neutral nations—Austria, Sweden and Switzerland—which Britain incidentally would have willingly approved as Sweden and Switzerland were two of her closest European trading partners and also among the most virile democracies anywhere. But the concept of a more liberal if looser West European economic grouping which would embrace the most traditionally democratic countries held no interest for Kennedy whatsoever. His primary interest in Western Europe was, as for the US State Department, as a bulwark against the Soviet bloc.

In his attempt to evolve a European identity which might one day stand aside from being a necessary part of either the American or Soviet hegemonies De Gaulle for one never lost sight of the pre-eminently military nature of US objectives in Europe as in every continent of the world. Thus De Gaulle took exception to the Nassau agreement for Britain to obtain Polaris nuclear submarines not, as Macmillan believed, because Britain had succeeded in preserving her independence, but because in France's view Britain had lost it. When De Gaulle exercised his veto in January 1963 he was infinitely more concerned about the extension of US predominance to a prospective partner in the EEC than about any overtones of British subservience. If Edward Heath was later to put Britain very much in pawn to France in the person of Georges Pompidou, the then French President saw Macmillan, not to put too fine a point upon it, as the willing but unwitting stooge of American strategic interests. With some precision the General saw the maintenance of the Anglo-American connection as at least in part an American device to influence Europe. Britain thus became in a very practical manner the victim of De Gaulle's anti-American Europeanism. Yet the General may fairly be said to have been right in appreciating that such arrangements as Nassau were incompatible with a "European" Europe, by which he meant a continentalized Europe which would one day stretch from the Atlantic to the Urals.

But the American plan (one might fairly call it the Ball Plan) to assist British entry into the EEC in whatever way possible would not have been effective in the end, as it ultimately proved to be, had it not been for the systematic suppression of alternatives to British entry. Before examining what might have proved the most readily available alternative, it is essential to put the record straight after such a damning critique of the Anglo-American connection. One must therefore state that when each partner takes into account the true interests of the other, rather than the overriding interests of the stronger, the Anglo-American relationship is an indispensable partnership to both countries, to the world, and, not least, to Western Europe as two world wars testify.

Among the chief and most appealing of the alternatives to British entry were the proposals for the creation of a North Atlantic Free Trade Area (NAFTA), a linking of the seven members of EFTA with the United States and Canada and probably Australia and New Zealand. If such a trading bloc should prove its worth, and once created there is no reason why such a group should not confer great benefits on all its members without harming any third parties, then it would be perfectly feasible for such a grouping to invite the original Six members of the EEC to join NAFTA in due course. So the argument for NAFTA ran. By making the principles of a liberal trading system the basic common denominator for such an association, rather than the boundaries of Western Europe, NAFTA would have represented a much more modern and flexible framework to deal with such contemporary world problems as monetary reform, energy and agriculture. Moreover, it would represent the coming together, in a loose framework, of the world's most mature democratic states without creating any centralized bureaucratic superstate structure. Though the concept of NAFTA as an alternative to British entry to the EEC enjoyed its greatest vogue in the period from 1967 to 1970, its origins go back as far as the beginning of World War II—the same period which saw Winston Churchill offer common citizenship to the French people in the war against the Nazis.

In 1940 James Meade, later to become Professor of Economics at Cambridge University, enunciated the principles of NAFTA in a paper he prepared for the British Government. It took another twenty-two years before Professor Meade produced a Hobart Paper for the Institute of Economic Affairs, expanding his original concept. Five years later, or more than a quarter of a century after Meade had first conceived the idea, after the second de Gaulle veto, NAFTA suddenly became, at least theoretically, a leading option.

Between 1967 and 1970 a group known as the Atlantic Trade Study group promoted its virtues. The ATS, founded by Hugh Corbet, a *Times* writer on international trade, Professor Harry Johnson, who held chairs in economics at both the London School of Economics and Chicago University, and the late Leonard Beaton, Director of Studies at the Institute of Strategic Studies, met regularly at Rules Restaurant. Subsequently it spawned the Trade Policy Research Centre and the British North America Committee. Its advocates included for a time Lord Watkins, former Minister of Defence, and Sir Frederick Catherwood, the then highly active and effective Director-General of the National Economic Development Council (NEDDY). Catherwood remembers that Dr Kissinger said as late as 1971 that if the British entry bid failed then NAFTA would certainly be seriously explored as one of the alternatives. There is even a suspicion that though by 1968 it would have been difficult for the United States to reverse its previous support for British entry Kissinger took a much more sceptical and pragmatic view of its precise benefits for Britain, Europe and especially the United States. If the Six were continually at loggerheads on matters of foreign policy would a Community of Ten (as first envisaged, before Norway voted to stay out) find a common voice on the selfsame issues, reasoned Kissinger. Meanwhile as far back as 1967, after Prime Minister Harold Wilson had been wooed by President Johnson (see the chapter on the Labour Party) he requested Catherwood to ease off his promotion of NAFTA. Catherwood's speech to the Foreign Affairs Club in 1967 for instance was called off. Had President Johnson in effect said to the British Prime Minister that British entry into the EEC was the only live alternative, or was it more of a response to the unpleasant aroma of Vietnam and the sensitivity of the Prime Minister to being too closely associated with the Americans by the Left wing of the Labour Party? It was probably a combination of the two factors. Undoubtedly Vietnam muddied the waters for both the British and American advocates of NAFTA.

Having examined the general posture of the American Government towards Britain in the postwar period, its promotion of British entry and its foreclosure of the chief alternative, it may be useful to summarize the ingredients of the Anglo-American connection. President Kennedy, himself a World War II veteran

and the successor to a President who had been the Supreme
Allied Commander in Europe in both war and peace, was
deeply aware of the value of the Anglo-American relationship
to the United States. Not only was its existence crucial to the
success of the allies in both world wars but it provided the essential cornerstone of NATO. While a close partnership with the
United States helped to preserve Britain's worldwide influence
it was more than passingly useful to the American strategic
interest. Paradoxically, while America wished to break up the
Commonwealth preference system it wanted the military lifelines
which accompanied it, particularly East of Suez, fully
maintained.

If the benefits for Britain were chiefly military and secondarily
diplomatic, the benefits for the United States were in having an
ally with a genuinely global view of events. This was not surprising given that the Pax Americana was succeeding the Pax
Brittanica. Nevertheless the Americans, for quite solid reasons,
not least financial, were anxious that Britain should continue her
global military role. Gradually it became apparent that Britain
simply could not sustain such commitments. The solution which
gradually developed among strategists at the State Department
incorporated the view that Europe would replace Britain as
America's chief ally. Moreover, as such, Europe, or more precisely the EEC countries, might in time supplant British influence
in Africa, Asia, Australasia, the Caribbean and the Middle East
and assume responsibility for the British bases in the Far East,
the Indian Ocean, the Persian Gulf and the Mediterranean. It
was a forlorn hope.

It is not difficult in such circumstances to argue that the
United States, by encouraging a continuing British military
presence East of Suez, by repeatedly bailing Britain out financially, by insisting that Britain defend the pound at a fixed rate
rather than allowing it to float in 1966, reinforced British
incapacity to deal with its own economic weakness, both structural and psychological, and ultimately hastened the decline in
national self-confidence. This is clearly manifested in the erosion
of Britain's democratic institutions and the growing belief that
Britain could not survive outside the EEC that has been described
in previous chapters.

While George Ball never tired in pointing out that the Anglo-
American relationship was a constant affront to France, whose
government Kennedy attempted to mollify by calling her

"America's oldest ally", the relationship was a genuine one forged in the maelstrom of two world wars. As one of Kennedy's men put it very succinctly : "We hoped that if England went into Europe it would take a sense of the 'special relationship' with it and that we would then have a special relationship with Europe." It was a simple case of transference. The illogicality and plain naivety of this belief, however well-intentioned, does not disguise the fact that it was central to the Kennedy Grand Alliance and underlay all the subsequent efforts for the next decade by successive US administration to expedite Britain's entry into the EEC.

The obvious question must eventually arise; how is it that the United States, the champion of the "free world" and leader of the western democracies, should have been so persistently active in arranging the affairs of her chief democratic allies in Western Europe? In the sense that the United States has had a political, economic and above all military stake in Europe's future the answer to that question has been to some extent sketched in the preceding pages. But there is a constitutional or structural question that also needs answering.

We have already seen how the United States fatally forced the pace in the creation of the embryo European Defence Community, largely because she failed to take account of the peoples as distinct from the governments involved. In a limited sense the affair illustrates one of the glaring weaknesses of US policy formulation towards Europe. Namely, that whereas, as Professor Max Beloff points out,[2] American foreign policy had in general terms to achieve popular domestic support, or at least acquiescence through the constitutional processes of Congressional committees open to the press, "in Europe it was thought to be sufficient to make bargains with existing governments". Thus from the very outset of the postwar period, as we have seen, US economic assistance to Europe was predicated on the assumption that it would further European integration "of some sort". Certainly Hubert Humphrey, a man with a very acute political antennae, thought as much and so told the Strasbourg Conference with more candour than most of the Congressional delegates who attended. But it was John Foster Dulles himself who put America's aims in typically blunt terms : "The hands-off policy has not succeeded and we face a choice between exerting pres-

[2] Max Beloff, *Foreign Policy and the Democratic Process*, John Hopkins Press.

sure to get done what needs to be done or acquiescing in a continuing disunity."

The sentiments have been shared, if not openly expressed, by every succeeding Secretary of State. Secretary Kissinger, although he is a much more subtle and sophisticated diplomatist than Dulles ever purported to be, has nevertheless accepted such tenets as implicit in the role of a super-power—it would be sheer folly to refrain from acting upon them. Whether in his role as a member of the National Security Council or of such sub-committees as the Forty Committee, the current US Secretary of State has been the most actively successful in deploying the full panoply of American power. His deployment and/or skilful co-ordination of the chief organs of the US Government ranging from the State Department, the Treasury, the Commerce Department, the Departments of the Navy, Army and Air Force, and, last but not least, the Central Intelligence Agency have been indispensable to the effectiveness of his structural as distinct from his personal diplomacy.

What emerges from this chapter is the sheer irreversible momentum that foreign policy acquires once it has been set in motion and pursued persistently for a period of years. It is my basic contention that the United States, by the single-minded pursuit of legitimate, even worthy, foreign policy goals in Europe, created both the general preconditions and the climate which helped to predispose Britain to enter the EEC at some future date —no more and no less than that.

CONCLUSION

> In a progressive country change is constant; and the question is not whether you should resist change which is inevitable, but whether that change should be carried out in deference to the manners, the customs, the laws, and the traditions of a people, or whether it should be carried out in deference to abstract principles and arbitrary and general doctrines.

THESE MUCH QUOTED words taken from a speech made by Disraeli in Edinburgh in 1867 are pertinent to the short narrative of events which we have now completed. One must judge for oneself to what extent Britain's entry into the Common Market was carried out in deference to the manners, customs, laws and traditions of the British people or was carried out in deference to principles and doctrines subscribed to by a relatively small minority. It is the author's conviction that while the organic structures of British democracy were far from being by-passed, they were to a very considerable extent manipulated from within to serve the aims and purposes of a determined if high-minded élite of top bureaucrats in both government and industry. While the nature of that alliance can be deduced from the events described in the preceding chapters there is a need to spell out such a thesis in more general terms.

For very nearly thirty years Britain's declining economic performance has been catalogued in some detail and its causes analysed from both a technical and psychological viewpoint. It is part of the record of this book that for at least half that period of gradual but increasing economic and political decline the vision of British entry into the Common Market has been the one transcending overall solution which has preoccupied top civil service bureaucrats and captains of industry alike.

The civil servants, and above all the officials of the Foreign Office, part of a structure which was inherited from the Victorian period when Britain was the hub of a great imperial system, saw in the emerging European Economic Community a means of preserving a great-power role for Britain and promoting it as a very contemporary expression of post-war internationalism. The reality was something quite different, namely that stripped of her empire Britain was never again to be a great power and that the EEC, far from being an example of post-war internationalism represented West European nationalism in a regional guise. Once the transitional period of "reparations" to France had been completed (most notably in the form of the common Agricultural Policy) there could be only one eventual leader within the Community, West Germany, gradually ascendant in both political as well as economic power and slowly arousing the fears of the Soviet bloc. Rather than accepting a middle-sized power or Elizabethan role, Britain, by opting for the Community, was clinging to its Victorian self-image.

The captains of industry, deeply aware that Britain's economic performance was deteriorating, saw accurately enough that paucity of investment was a fundamental factor in Britain's poor record. As we have already seen, the EEC offered to them the prospect, or so it seemed, of a greatly expanded home market and a maximization of flexibility in the deployment of capital and labour throughout the EEC, advantages that the US multinational companies had been exploiting for some time. In the first year of British membership British companies invested £330m on Britain's Continental partners who invested only £45m in return.

Though their visions were different, these two influential groups, standing respectively at the pinnacle of the public and private bureaucracies, made common cause in a goal that was represented as being in the national interest. The alliance on the Common Market over these last fifteen years illustrates a very basic change which took place during this same period, the evolution of the corporatist state, that is, one where private ownership exists under state control. This is in addition to the more than 50 per cent of the British economy already under state control employing 30 per cent of the national labour force —i.e. nearly 8 million out of 25 million. The bureaucracies of the public and private sectors have come more and more to merge with one another, as the elimination of competition in return for state support proceeded steadily under Conservative and Labour governments alike.

As the chapter on the Civil Service tends to corroborate, the doctrine of ministerial responsibility, and its attendant concept of accountability to Parliament and press, is no more than a myth. With something of the order of 700,000 civil servants and around 70 Ministers it has for some time appeared a doctrine extremely difficult to sustain in practice. That the transfer of both political and administrative power on an unprecedented scale to Brussels would do anything but hasten the transfer of effective political power from parliamentary to bureaucratic institutions, whether they be Commissions, Councils or multinational companies, is simply not credible. It may go some way to explaining the enthusiasm of the British bureaucrats in both Whitehall and in private industry, more especially big business, for the Common Market structures that already exist. Indeed, no less person than Ralf Dahrendorf, notable as the most liberally minded and progressive EEC Commissioner in the Community's history, was reported as saying at Königswinter as late as 1975 that there is very little future in national parliaments. The real question facing the British people in 1975 was not so much whether the renegotiation of British entry terms were satisfactory or not but whether the decline of the traditional British parliamentary system was inevitable or whether it could be reversed.

But Britain's obsession with gaining entry to the EEC as a solution to her national problems, both psychological and material, was no mere outgrowth of the Civil Service and big business lobbies, or even of their respective oligarchies. It was also a chimera pursued prior to 1973 by what were then each of the three major political parties. It was, one suspects, because Britain's leaders were to a greater or lesser extent unable to accept, or more precisely to persuade their respective parties to accept, the diminished status of a middle-sized power that Britain suffered a succession of failures. With each failure national morale suffered a further blow. In time both major political parties, or at least their leaders, saw Britain's joining of the Common Market as not only a new great-power role for Britain to play but also a form of political and economic panacea for Britain's post-war malaise. The Liberal Party has stoutly maintained its ideal of the Common Market as an extension of classical liberal free trade principles despite the fact that its twin instruments of the Common Agricultural Policy and the Common External Tariff reveal it to be the supreme manifestation of modern mercantilism.

The essential reality in 1975 was that whether Britain belonged or did not belong to the EEC, the foremost problems that she and all the countries of Western Europe faced were those of inflation, unemployment, energy, food and raw materials, to none of which did the institutions of the EEC bear any special relevance. Indeed, it is arguable that the Community's structures constituted a handicap in each of these fields. The classic example of the Community revealing its inherent structural weakness, affecting each of these issues, was in the wake of the October 1973 Middle East war when the Community for all practical purposes fell apart, its national divisions contrasting markedly with the much more loosely allied members of the rump of EFTA who presented a virtually united front. Since few people would discount the possibility of another Middle East war and there is well nigh universal agreement that the other issues are likely to remain with us for some time, there is a good case for applying a hearty dose of political pragmatism rather than for Britain binding herself too closely to a bureaucratic structure of doubtful resilience. The prospect of the Nine bickering over minor institutional reforms and common standards while their social and democratic institutions are swept away (having already been seriously eroded) in a wave of hyper-inflation and its handmaiden of massive unemployment is not so improbable that it can be totally discounted.

Instead of the syndrome of Britain behaving like some Byronic sad mother of a dead empire yearning for her imperial youth, the prospect of regular collaboration with most if not all the countries of Western Europe in an industrial free trade area is already to hand—with the added advantage of not discriminating against any of Britain's prospective trade partners outside Europe. By contrast the vision of a politically united Western European bloc is as distant as ever. Indeed, it is the EEC alternative that is the least clear, since nobody knows what kind of political structure will eventually evolve and more particularly what democratic checks, if any, will ultimately emerge. Whether Britain opts for the looser, more flexible alternative of West European collaboration with its retention of parliamentary sovereignty, or the centralized bureaucratic alternative, she will still be left with solving her own internal problems for which no external arrangement will provide more than a temporary respite. With the need to batten down her economic and social hatches to withstand the exigencies of a siege economy for the next few years Britain can no longer escape the stark truth that the path immediately ahead will not be a smooth one. The paramount question is : will Britain's people be so convinced that they have chosen the right path that they will pull together ?

The last word must lie with Dr Henry Kissinger who wrote with some prescience in *A World Restored* (Gollancz, 1974) : "The test of a statesman is his ability to recognise the real relationship of forces and to make this knowledge serve his ends. . . . The acid test of a policy, however, is its ability to obtain domestic support." At no moment in its history since the Act of Union did this statement apply so pertinently to the United Kingdom, to both its political leadership and its future social cohesion, as in 1975.